PRECIOUS MEMORIES
LEGACY

Stories and Memories of Country Music Legends told by their Kids

RENAE JOHNSON

ISBN: 978-0-692-57467-6

Renae The Waitress, LLC
PO Box 210796
Nashville, TN 37221

www.RenaetheWaitress.com
www.PreciousMemoriesMemorial.com

2

Special Thanks to all of these great kids for their time and photo contributions. I hope this book not only honors them, but also continues to keep their parents memory alive.

And a **VERY SPECIAL THANK YOU**… to Robyn Young who totally inspired me to put this book together and to Paula Winters who not only helped but also cheered me on!! And of course my hero in Australia, Steve Williams @ Red Inc. who takes my messy and bossy instructions and creates a great book!! You rock!

Other books by Renae Johnson
Diary of a TV Waitress
Precious Memories Memorial

*I*ntroduction

While writing my book *Precious Memories Memorial* I kept thinking about the families of theses country music legends who have passed away. What was it like for the kids? Did they grieve and miss these legends in my book? Or did they grieve and miss a parent?

These Legends were raised in a different era where working hard and making sacrifices were all they knew. Most of them were raised poor and they were raised to love God and Country. Taking the opportunity to better their lives and providing more for their kids by doing what they loved was a dream. They became bigger than life to their fans but who were they to their kids? Legend or Parent?

I decided to ask nineteen kids all the same questions. Ten questions exactly. Some of the answers became stories that are funny and light hearted while some are sad and heart wrenching. There seems to be a common thread that weaves through all their lives…. Missed birthdays, holidays and special moments that could not be given back. But there is no mistake they would not have traded their lives for anyone else.

eet the Kids…

Robyn Young * son of Faron Young, *Ronny Robbins* * son of Marty Robbins, *Becky Ashworth* * daughter of Ernie Ashworth, *Jett Williams* * daughter of Hank Williams, *Hawkshaw Hawkins Jr.* * son of Hawkshaw Hawkins and Jean Shepard, *Julie Husky* * daughter of Ferlin Husky, *Melissa Luman* * daughter of Bob Luman, *Georgette Jones* * daughter of George Jones and Tammy Wynette, *Kim Brown* * daughter of Jim Ed Brown, *Michael Twitty* * son of Conway Twitty, *Dean Miller* * son of Roger Miller, *Chrystie Wooley* * daughter of Sheb Wooley, *Sharon Wilburn* * daughter of Doyle Wilburn, *Lisa Anderson* * daughter of Lynn Anderson, *Jesse Keith Whitley* * son of Keith Whitley and Lorrie Morgan, *Steve Kilgore* * son of Merle Kilgore, *Kathy Louvin* * daughter of Ira Louvin. *George Hamilton V* * son of George Hamilton IV, *Seidina Reed* * daughter of Jerry Reed.

Visit Facebook: Next Generation: Son's & Daughters of Country Legends for performance schedules.

Contents

Robyn Young

1

The new Country Music Entertainers will leave a different kind of *Legacy* than your father had the opportunity to leave. How comfortable do you feel with today's Country Music?

The really new ones, if you put a gun to my head and told me to name whoever the new hoo-hah artists are... I wouldn't know. I don't listen to them and couldn't name a song. I try and turn it on every once in a while... and I have to just turn it off. It just doesn't check with me. I'm the kinda guy who grew up around Dad, and Brenda Lee, and Ernest Tubb, Web Pierce and Lefty Fizzell and all these people. People laugh all the time when I talk about this new breed of country singers, Reba, George Strait, Larry Gatlin. They all look at me like "What? Man, they're old-timers"... Not to me. I didn't really have a problem with Waylon and Willie and the outlaw movement. I liked all that. The Gatlins I loved, and Ronnie Milsap and Ricky Skaggs. But now, it's moved in a direction that does not connect with me at all. I grew up with a totally different type of country music. First of all, there is no steel guitar or fiddle on any songs anymore. That's like knocking the hat off the Pope or something... you don't get to see the Pope again with the funny hat... know what I mean?

Faron

2

As a child of a Country Music legend what do you feel was the biggest event or experience that impacted *you* the most growing up?

You know, I knew my dad was a country singer, and we had gone to the Opry a couple of times when I was a little kid. I knew by around second grade that there was something a little different when the teachers in my school were coming up to me, asking me to get them things, like autograph albums from Dad, and they weren't asking other kids... you know. Probably the single biggest event happened when I was maybe 4 or 5 years old - no older than that - and Dad took me and my older brother (of which we were the only two children at that time. The younger kids hadn't come along yet) to the Grand Ole Opry. It was at the Ryman, and we were sitting down in the front row with Mom; it might have been the first time I'd ever gone to the Opry. And we were sitting there watching Dad. Dad was up there doing his thing, and looked down and all of a sudden said "Come 'mere... come 'mere, give him to me."... I was like "What?"

Then I realized that he was asking Mom to hand me up to him. She handed me up to him and he grabbed me while he was singing a song, and I was totally terrified being up there. I ended up peeing in my pants. He sat me down and then handed me back down to Mom, but I remember being terrified getting up there in front of all those people. It was years later when I was singing on my own that I went back to the Opry and finally got a shot at the new Opry House, and I am proud to say that I did way better that time... I actually came off the stage dry. So it was a definite improvement for me.

3

Let's talk more about your life behind the curtain. So many of the Country singers were on the road most of the time. Share with me life at home with or without your father. How did that form your life's decisions and path?

In my early years was when my dad was really super hot... I mean he was one of the hottest guys out there in country music at the time, which naturally corresponds with the fact that he wasn't home a lot. Because he could go out and play all of those dates, that is ultimately why he, Kitty Wells, and some of these other people got dropped off of the Opry: because they weren't meeting their requirements. Of course, it's funny how those requirements do not apply to Garth and Reba and all of those people anymore. But back then, they actually got dropped off of the Opry roster because of it. I think you made $17.50 for doing songs on the Opry, but you could go out and make a couple thousand on the road. So it was a no-brainer what they were going to do. He was gone a lot, so it put a lot of burden on my mom, and I am close to my mom. I had a great mom who stepped up and did a lot of stuff, and made sure that we were covered on stuff, because a lot of times, on our birthdays Dad wasn't there. She made sure we got a birthday party and things like that. Now there were some kids, like Charlie Louvin's kids, who went to my school; and Shelly West, Dottie West's daughter, and all of Dottie's kids went to my school. So there were some whom I grew up around, but most of my friends were kids whose dads worked in offices, sold insurance or something like that.

That was kinda the weird thing: you don't know that something is different, or that you're missing anything. When you're a kid, you're happy-go-lucky and you don't have bills to pay… you're just out to have fun. But I would go to my friends' houses on the weekend to spend the night, and I would be amazed that their dads were there. "Wow, your dad's home?" "Well… yeah." "Every weekend?" "Yeah…" "Oh wow, my dad is never home on a weekend." I was a little jealous. But when I got around the other kids of entertainers, it was a shared experience with all of us that we could understand. It was funny that our other friends always thought we were rich, and that we were just born with a silver spoon in our mouths. Like when we would all get together and go to mall, they would say "Let Robyn buy it, he's rich… his dad is a country singer". Ya'll haven't met my dad! My dad was not a big time spender… he was a very thrifty person. We had an 8 ½ acre yard on Hillsboro Rd., where the buses of "See the Homes of the Stars" came by, so it had to look good for those people. Dad wouldn't hire a lawn crew. You can see Mexicans and Trucks running everywhere with lawn mowers in Tennessee now. But back in

9

those days, it was just me and my brother, and it was a big deal when Dad started giving us $5.00 apiece for cutting the grass. 8 ½ acres manicured. I have been asked this question forever: "What was it like having a big star as a father?" What it really meant was that you didn't see your dad a lot.

What single song was your favorite? Why?

There are a lot of them I like by my dad. I like the 4/4 shuffles and the twin fiddles that he did a lot in his Mercury Records years. He did an album when I was really young called *"Faron Young Aims at the West"*. It was all cowboy songs; it had *Streets of Laredo*, the theme song from Bonanza, and all these classic cowboy songs. He had one called *Yellow Bandana* that was written for him. And that was my older brother's favorite song, as well as mine. We used to wear that album out, 'cause we thought cowboys were cool. We watched Roy Rogers and knew that our dad was "The Singing Sheriff". We were into the cowboy thing; but we had no idea what a

bandana was until later, when Willie Nelson wore it around his head. So we called it the "Yellow Banana", and thought that was the name of the song, and we always said "Daddy, sing the *Yellow Banana* song for us".

5

What other entertainers were you close to growing up? Who hung around your house?

No body on a regular basis because dad was gone and most of the time when he hung out with his pals it would be down at his office. There were times I can remember when Brenda Lee coming over for Dinner, I can remember Willie coming over. Webb and his wife Audrey they would come over from time to time. Lefty Frizzell was out there one day when dad was trying to teach me to ride a bicycle without training wheels. Lefty ended up sending dad to the house. Lefty stayed with me until I learned to ride my bike. Now how many kids can say they learned to ride a bike with the help of Lefty Frizzell.

6

In the story of *your* life, what memories do you have of holidays and special events with your father?

A lot of times, especially back in his days, like New Years, he was gone. But most of the time he was home for Christmas. He was not there for a lot of my birthdays, but usually on Christmas they would schedule to be home; but sometimes, maybe the day after, he would have to leave, because they had to head across the country. He might be playing for New Years, maybe at the Palomino Club out in Bakersfield.

A lot of the holidays like New Years were the nights that you wanted to be on the road, because you got paid double.

One of the special Christmases, I guess I would have been about 6. I got my first guitar. Dad got me a guitar, and it was a Harmony with a red and black kind of sunburst. It was one of those guitars that doesn't have the hole in the middle. It has the violin-styled F-shaped holes on the side, with a kind of arch stop.

And actually, even though it was a cheap guitar for a kid and beginner guitar back then, that guitar (in good condition) would now actually be worth a little bit of money. So I remember getting that, and then by the next Christmas, I had already convinced myself that I was the world's greatest guitar player, and that I was way above that cheap guitar that he had gotten me. The good thing back then was that Fender, Shure, Gibson and other brands would outfit artists. They would outfit dad and his entire band with new instruments every year so that they could run articles in the magazines saying things like "Faron Young sings on Shure microphones", or "Faron Young plays Fender guitars". So a lot of times when they would re-outfit them, they wouldn't make them give the other stuff back. So for Christmas, I would be like "Dad, I want a electric guitar and amp" and I would end up getting Odale Martin's old guitar that he had been playing for the year, and it would be like a 65 Fender stratocaster and a Fender Super Reverb with four 10" JBL speakers in it. You would have to go pawn your house nowdays to buy them. So those were some of the fringe benefits of you know… "Dad isn't going to be here for Christmas, but you got a killer guitar."

7

I love dogs and had a blonde Cocker Spaniel growing up. Please tell me about *your* pets, if any, or *your* pet as a child.

Growing up as the child of Faron Young, it is heartbreaking to have to tell you about pets. My mom actually got onto him at one point. My dad kinda loved animals… he grew up on a dairy farm, but of course he wasn't home to take care of them.

But dad loved cute little puppies. So dad would go out and buy puppies, and probably the first one was a cute little Collie puppy who we named Ladd. We fell in love with Ladd, and played with him and had a doghouse. About six months later, Dad comes in and Ladd is not a cute little adorable fuzzy puppy anymore. Ladd is like a full-grown dog! So Dad would give it away to somebody and go buy another puppy. He got a little pug, and we named him Mr. Peabody, and we loved Mr. Peabody, and then Mr. Peabody made the mistake of

turning into a dog. And dad got rid of it, and went out and got something else. And mom finally told him "Faron, you have to quit doing this." And he said "Well, I like a cute little puppy."

Then mom said "Yeah, but the kids love these dogs. They're around them every day, and they get attached to them. And then you go and get rid of them, and they come home and their hearts are broken." And he just said "Oh… I didn't realize that… I thought they'd like getting a new puppy." He'd brought home a couple of Teacup Chihuahas. But she finally broke him of that. I think it was an honest mistake I don't think he thought we were crushed when we came home and Mr. Peabody was gone. So I had several, but my favorite pet as a child was back when Dad had an office on Music Row. He was one of the first country artists to have their office building on Music Row. There were record companies, and he was doing good back then, so he built this office. When he expanded the building and added three stories to it, they got this dog that was part Timber Wolf and part German Shepherd, and they put it out in the yard where they had all the construction materials. And this dog would eat you alive. The building was on Division, and back in that day you had rich Music Row 16th and 17th Ave., then a few streets over would be impoverished poor people in the next streets over from it.

It was weird, the difference in money and people just a few streets over. So there was crime up around Music Row, and they needed this guard dog. But once they got the building done and didn't need the dog there anymore, they needed to get rid of it. Since Dad was one of the few people who could get around it without it attacking, he ended up bringing it home. He told us "Don't go out by the dog. I'm gonna put it out on the patio and let him see you through the window for a few days... let it get used to you... 'cause this dog could hurt you." And I'm kinda like "yeah, yeah, yeah". I've always loved dogs, so as soon as Dad walked out of the room I headed out there and started playing with it. And the dog took to me. They had never named it, so I named it Barron Von Farron. We just called him Barron for short, and he was a great dog and my favorite. But he didn't like strangers, and we would have

to put him up or tie him up whenever someone came over, and that ended up being his doom. Dad's manager came over unannounced once, and the dog was out and evidently bit a tire and got too close, and ultimately got ran over. He was a trained guard dog, but he loved me to death.

8

Explain to me how you were able to share *your* musical talents with your father. If not, how have you shared your talents with his fans?

I worked for him for a year or so out on the road from time to time, especially at Dad's club; I would play with his band. I went out with him on the road and opened his shows. That was a great time for us and we had even talked about doing an ablum together. He needed another album and that would have been a good lick for me. But then the divorce happened, and all of that got put on the back burner, and we never really got back moving on it. I really regret that.

When I would travel with him on the road, he would bring me out and I would do my thing and then he would come out and we would sing together. When Ralph Emery had *"Nashville Now"*, I was on there 8 or 10 times. About half of those appearances were by myself and half of them were with Dad. A lot of times, we would do *"Wind Me Up"* and *"Alone with You"*. I've still got some of the old videos, and some of those are on YouTube.

I tell you what's kinda funny: like I get around Michael Twitty, who's a good friend of mine. Michael always talks about Conway. "My daddy was the best dad that there ever was. My dad was so loving and such a good person." And then I would get around Kim Corwan, who is Jim Ed Brown's daughter, who I call KIM ED Brown. Jim Ed was one of the sweetest people ever, and she is still mourning her father. It hasn't been that long. And she gets real torn up and says, "My dad was the sweetest man, and such an inspiration."

What do you miss most about your father?

What I miss most about my dad are the routines and hell-

raising stuff that he did. My dad was buck wild. A lot of people were kinda scared to death to play with him. There were even musicians who would go on the road and work for him one weekend and then quit. "Ah… Faron scares me. I can't be out there!"

I remember hearing stories about things he had done, and about how wild his band was on the road. And when I was younger, I couldn't wait to get to go out on the road with him. I'd bet it was going to be a non-stop party all the time. But when I finally got out on the road, they had slowed down and it wasn't that big rock n roll lifestyle that I thought it would be. Now there was some partying sometimes, but a lot time there wasn't.

My dad… he didn't fit into the fathership role all that well. He didn't fit into the husband role very well at all. And there were some things he did just as a man that I was a little disappointed in, and I kinda looked to my grandfather as being a better example of what a man should be like. But he was one hell of a country singer. He was legendary for his hell-raising. You can't go anywhere in this town and not run into people that will tell you just a GREAT story about Faron Young.

Waylon and Johnny Cash would both come up to you and tell you great stories that were legendary about my father and things that he'd done. For a guy who was a little man and kinda had a Napoleonic Complex, and kinda had a chip on his shoulder about people who where bigger than him, he lived really BIG. He was exciting, but that's what made him kinda dangerous. When things were slowing down for him and other country performers, I asked Dad's manager why he didn't get him on the Opry again, and he said "Robyn, they don't want him… they are scared to death of him. That's a live show that goes out to family audiences, and they don't know if Faron's gonna show up drunk or get up and cuss out someone in the front row." So a lot of his wildness that made him legendary actually hurt him towards the end of his career. Not that they didn't think he could potentially have more hits, but they had heard all of the wild stories and were afraid of having him on the record label. They didn't necessarily want a wild man… they wanted somebody they could control.

Do you have a website or Facebook page you would like to share?

On my website and Facebook page there is a lot of stuff about my dad, but also stuff about my great-great grandfather on my mother's side… Uncle Dave Macon, who was the FIRST star of the Grand Ole Opry. He was the guy who used to come out and sit in a rocking chair and play the banjo, and had a mouth full of gold teeth. And his son, Doris, would play guitar with him. His other son's son was my grandfather Robert, who was a decorated veteran and, meaning no disrespect to my dad, but he was the greatest man I ever knew. Grandpa taught me about being a man, and he taught me to have respect for our country. I couldn't have had anyone better to fill in and be there for me.

Facebook: Robynyoungartist

Website: www.robynyoung.band

Michael Twitty

1

The new Country Music Entertainers will leave a different kind of *Legacy* than your father had the opportunity to leave. How comfortable do you feel with today's Country Music?

Not "comfortable" at all. I don't care for what NASHVILLE is cranking out today and calling it "Country", aside from a handful of artists that are still doing traditional Country. When I started out in Country Music back in '72, Dad said "You're gonna have to get some 'age' on you before Country fans will accept you.

Right now, they just aren't gonna take you seriously, because you're not old enough yet to understand the things that you are singing about!" Today, you're "too old" if you're past 30 or so, and Nashville caters to the young people and they have turned their backs on millions of traditional Country fans. *"Murder has been committed down on Music Row"*. True song, without a doubt.

2

As a child of a Country Music legend what do you feel was the biggest event or experience that impacted *you* the most growing up?

Conway

Any time I was on stage with Dad was very special, as well as every release of a new album, as I would sit with my guitar and learn every word and every chord of every song. Dad taught me my first few chords, and I kinda took it from there. I was, and am, a huge fan of his music, in addition to being his son.

Let's talk more about your life behind the curtain. So many of the Country singers were on the road most of the time. Share with me life at home with or without your father. How did that form your life's decisions and path?

I am my father's only child by his first marriage. I wound up being raised by his Mother and Father, in the very same place that he was raised: the "Delta" of Mississippi. In THAT way, we were "brothers", as well as father and son. I loved my grandparents VERY much. Papaw was a riverboat pilot on the Mississippi River, and Mamaw ran our restaurant on Moon Lake called "Conways". I kinda had a "Huck Finn"

type of raisin'. The roots of my raisin' run very deep.

— 4 —

What single song was your favorite? Why?

It's Only Make Believe. It kept Dad in the music business! After YEARS of recording and traveling, doing live shows, he just wasn't "hitting it big". So after he'd written *"Make Believe"*, he said "If this song doesn't make it, I quit!" Well, it didn't, and he DID quit and move back home to Helena, Arkansas.

Months later though, he received a call from a DJ in Ohio, asking him to come do a show, because he had the hottest record in Columbus! Well, Dad threw the old band back together, jumped into an old station wagon with a U-Haul trailer behind it and headed to Ohio, where thousands of screaming teenagers greeted him! The rest, as they say, is history. Thank God for that song, or the world may never have gotten to enjoy "Conway Twitty"!

5

What other entertainers were you close to growing up? Who hung around your house?

Well, growing up in the Delta, I only saw Dad when he would come through on tour, either to eat at the restaurant or to play a show there, as we had bands come in on the weekends. However, I got to meet the artists and spend time with them then (being on tour with dad), as well as when they worked "Conways" themselves. Loretta Lynn was always super sweet to me; I still call her "Momma Loretta" today. I must admit, I was very close to my Dad's drummer Tommy "Porkchop" Markham, too. He bought me my first gas-powered model airplane and taught me to fly it. He was a great guy to me. I NEVER had a "shortage" of attention. ALL the artists, and their band members, were always very nice to me.

6

In the story of *your* life, what memories do you have of holidays and special events with your father?

Again, MY story is a little "different", being raised in the delta by Mamaw & Papaw, but my dad called all the time, and came by whenever he could. I must say that the most "exciting" times, though, were the times when he would play "Conways".

He always packed the house, and I would always sit in and sing with him. That was always very special to me, because I loved his music as well as the man. Great times.

7

I love dogs and had a blonde Cocker Spaniel growing up. Please tell me about *your* pets, if any, or *your* pet as a child.

I've always loved dogs. We have a little black & tan Chihuahua named "Gizmo". He was the "runt" of the litter, and was only the size of a pack of cigarettes at 6 weeks old! He weighs 6 pounds now, and is 16.5 years old. To my wife Barbie and me, he is our "baby"! Growing up, I always had dogs. We had thirteen

Beagles for hunting, as Papaw loved to do, and had taught me how to do as well. I also loved St. Bernards, and had several of them as well. I've just always been a dog lover! Not so much with cats, though, although I enjoy ALL animals.

8

Explain to me how you were able to share *your* musical talents with your father. If not, how have you shared your talents with his fans?

Well, I would always "sit in" with Dad whenever possible, of course... but a lot of times when he would visit, we would go out on our "pier" behind the cafe and sit and pick guitar, and sing songs together while fishing at the same time. These are some of my most treasured memories of childhood. It was very "special". As for his fans, I have shared his music and mine with them for my entire "professional life" since I first started in the music business, back in 1972. I've done shows in every State in the Union, including Alaska and Hawaii. I've also played in England, Germany, France, Nova Scotia, Newfoundland, Japan, and all across Canada. I've recorded for four major record labels, too. I really enjoy entertaining people, and it has been my life's work.

9

What do you miss most about your father?

Everything. His hugs, his smile, the tremendous love he had for me. I always knew that he was "there for me" if I needed him. Always. I miss him in EVERY way that it is possible to miss a human being, although I do feel him with me all the time.

I try to keep his memory alive with my show "Memories of Conway" that we do, which my son Tre is also part of. "That's My Job"!

10

Do you have a website or Facebook page you would like to share?

MichaelTwitty.Com is where the fans can keep up with me, as well as find my tour dates and check out my music videos.

Dean Miller

1

The new Country Music Entertainers will leave a different kind of *Legacy* than your father had the opportunity to leave. How comfortable do you feel with today's Country Music?

Most will leave no legacy, because they are making disposable music. I believe that they will have a short run, and that no one will remember them in ten years.

They are making music based on backwards corporate decisions instead of emotional, touching and deep thoughts. It used to be that a person wrote, and worked and crafted, and got better… and then continued to work on their craft, until one day when somebody would give them a chance and put some support behind them, and they would grow as a talent and entertainer. Now it works backwards. People in a corporate office say, "We need a blond guy, and let's find an artist who will fit our plan and mold them." I just don't think it works like it used to, and it's sad. I'd like to think that that's gonna change and come around. And I think it will… but for now, most current artists are not going to be remembered, in my opinion.

Roger

2

As a child of a Country Music legend, what do you feel was the biggest event or experience that impacted *you* the most growing up?

Man, I was aware from an early age that anything was possible, and that I did not have to fit into a mold or an idea of what other people thought was the right way to be or the right way to live. I saw things that most people aren't privileged enough to see and to know... anything is possible.

3

Let's talk more about your life behind the curtain. So many of the Country singers were on the road most of the time. Share with me life at home with or without your father. How did that form your life's decisions and path?

It had its ups and downs. There were times in my life where my dad was 100% there for me, and was the best dad ever. And there were also times he was absent. But in my teen years, I was able to travel with him more, and to be with him more and go on the road. And when I was able to follow his agenda, it was easier for me than if he'd had to stop and follow my agenda as a kid. But as a teenager, my life popped wide open, and I was able to be with my dad and follow him along on his travels and adventures.

4

What single song was your favorite? Why?

Can I say two things? *"King of the Road"*, because it paid for my existence, and *"Old Toy Trains"*, because it was written for and about me. To this day, I hear it every year at Christmastime, and it's always like my dad putting his arms around me and saying hello, and telling me that he loves me.

5

What other entertainers were you close to growing up? Who hung around your house?

Well, one of my dad's best friends in the whole world was Willie Nelson, so I spent a lot of time around him. Glen

Campbell and my dad were very close, so I spent a lot of time with him too. One time in high school, our driveway was about a quarter of a mile long. It was a dirt driveway out to the street, and I would always get dropped off at the school bus at the end of the road and walk up that driveway to our house. One day, I got dropped off from the school bus and there was a helicopter in our front field. Glen Campbell was playing Albuquerque, New Mexico, and we lived in Santa Fe. He had leased a helicopter and had flown it up to Santa Fe to see my dad, and he parked it out front. So it was pretty awesome to come home from school and see a helicopter and Glen Campbell waiting in your front yard. And the best part of the story is, Glen got lost, so they had landed the helicopter at a drug store. Glen got out and walked into the drug store and said, "Do you know where Roger Miller lives?" "Yeah… down the street, to the left." And so they followed the road to my dad's house in the helicopter. I often thought about those people in the drug store, who were probably thinking "what the heck?" when the helicopter landed and someone got out and asked for directions to Roger Miller's house!

6

In the story of *your* life, what memories do you have of holidays and special events with your father?

Holidays? You know, just being with my dad on holidays was a privilege. To be honest, he had seven kids from three different marriages, and I was the only kid that lived with him the most and was raised by him. So I think it was a privilege to be around him, and 90% of all of our Christmases were with my dad.

7

I love dogs and had a blonde Cocker Spaniel growing up. Please tell me about *your* pets, if any, or *your* pet as a child.

When I was born, my parents adopted a dog at the same time that I was born, so I had my own dog growing up, and then throughout my life I have always had dogs. Later on, I became a dog trainer/counselor, so the other half of my life was about dogs. One-half music and one-half dogs. And I have actually written a book about dogs called "A Dog's Way". I train, teach and counsel, and have developed my own method of training that I teach. So dogs are my whole life, they're my family.

8

Explain to me how you were able to share *your* musical talents with your father. If not, how have you shared your talents with his fans?

I started writing songs when I was about 13 or 14 years old. But when your father is one of the most revered songwriters in Country music and you say, "Hey, I wrote this little song", it's a little bit imitating. When you're young, most parents will just clap and say, "Oh, that's so good," and celebrate your every move, and think that every song is incredible. But my parents were both in music, so I would instead get, "Okay, that bridge needs work", "You're a little flat on this line", or "You should work on that word"... so that's what I got. Haha. It was a little bit different in my house when I began writing songs. I don't think that my dad lived long enough to see me get better or really good at it, but he taught

me so much about the craft of it. He was very good about that. And he was a big believer, and told me "Look… if this is going to mean anything to you, you're going to have to go out there and do this on your own. I can't hand it to you." So he didn't go make calls, and he didn't set up meetings. He didn't do anything to open doors, so I had to do it on my own. And at the time, it really made me mad, but as I got older I realized the value, and it made me a better singer, a better songwriter, and a better person.

9

What do you miss most about your father?

I miss his sense of humor the most. He was the funniest, and had the quickest wit of anybody that I ever met in my life. And I like that I inherited some of that. I LIVE for a well-crafted joke. LIVE FOR IT. So he and I shared that.

10

Do you have a website or Facebook page you would like to share?

Facebook.com/
Deanmillerpage
Deanmillerofficial.com
Deanmillerentertainment.com
Thedogcounselor.com

People always ask, "What kind of legacy did my father leave behind?" And I always tell them: "When I say his name to people, their whole face lights up." With a lot of people, you say their name and they go "Oh, that jerk", "Oh, that guy was mean", or "That guy messed me over". And when you say my father's name to anyone, they smile and their face lights up, and if they knew my dad they'll say, "Let me tell you a story". And then they'll tell a story of how he had an impact on their life. I think it's the most beautiful legacy that you can leave behind.

Seidina
Reed

1

The new Country Music Entertainers will leave a different kind of *Legacy* than your father had the opportunity to leave. How comfortable do you feel with today's Country Music?

Well, today's Country music is great music, but for the most part is really not "country". But the music business, it is a business, and they have to make money; and obviously that's what the young people want. It's more like Country Rock or Country Pop to me. But my dad… he's a legend. He's a history book guy. I am really proud of him. He was, first and foremost, an innovative, incredible guitar player. He called himself a "guitar thinker". As a singer-songwriter he was unique, and I don't see how there could ever be another one of him. Don't get me wrong, there is some good talent in Country Music today, but it's not true-blue Country. It's good, and I enjoy listening to it, and I am not putting it down at all. I'm not one of these grumpy old people who can't handle moving forward and progress. It happens. I am sure they went through this same thing in the beginning. When Country became more modern in the 60s and 70s, I am sure that folks were saying then "Oh… it ain't Country!" That's always happened, and so we are going through it again.

Jerry

2

As a child of a Country Music legend what do you feel was the biggest event or experience that impacted you the most growing up?

I can tell you my greatest experience was touring with Dad. I toured with Dad for years, musically speaking. When *Smokey and the Bandit* first came out, I was a teenager in high school, and I had no idea what the movie was about. So when we went to a private showing at the Belcout Theater, I laughed so hard I couldn't believe it. Back then, it was 100 Oaks and The Martin Theater… and I am giving away my age here, but I don't care, haha. So anyway, I went there to see it when it opened up in theaters, and it was packed. I was sitting right in the middle, and when Daddy ran over those motorcycles, everybody screamed and yelled, and so did I. We came outside after the movie and everyone was peeling out of the parking lot. That was a thrill for a teenage girl, but touring with Dad was just incredible. I learned a lot, and I really couldn't put into words what I learned, except that you are there to make people happy, and when you get

out on stage you need to have fun. You are an entertainer. So working with him made a tremendous impact on me, and I gained the greatest respect for my dad; because no matter how bad an artist feels, if you are on tour, you have to go out on that stage every night and you have to be on and happy, and you have to move that audience to feel something or to be happy as well. Anyone who can do that, no matter how bad they feel, is just amazing. Dad was unbelievable; he was always on, no matter how he felt or what he was dealing with. So that entire experience of working with my father was a great impact on me.

3

Let's talk more about your life behind the curtain. So many of the Country singers were on the road most of the time. Share with me life at home with or without your father. How did that form your life's decisions and path?

Well I was in music from the get-go. Back in those days, he was on the road all the time. Mama said one year that he had been home for two weeks out of the entire year. It was me going to school and eating Stover's frozen pizza with Mama on the bed, watching *Columbo* and *Murder She Wrote*. The rest of the time, I played the piano and was singing. That was me. But when Dad came home it was great. Funny! And he never stopped. He hit the floor running, always doing something. My greatest childhood memory of Dad being home was him always being in that kitchen, picking away on his guitar.

I got so used to hearing that beautiful guitar in the house that when I was out on my own, I missed that. Dad brought all the beauty and laughter into our family's life. He had a big life, and it left a big hole. My warmest memories were hearing that beautiful guitar and just DAD.

What single song was your favorite? Why?

I love *"Amos Moses"* 'cause he started writing it when I was a little girl. He always tried things out on me 'cause he said that I was his biggest fan. He sat on the fireplace, always stomping that foot. And he would say, "I'm writing a song, Pooky." He'd start playing in his Amos Moses little Cajun *"He lived by himself in the swamp"*, and then he would get to the part *"...and he'd just knock 'em in the head with a stomp..."* and this little 9-year-old kid here would roll in the floor laughing. So I loved that song, but there's another song of his, *"Mind Your Love"*, that I have always just adored. I sing that every year at the *Jerry Reed Celebration*, and I also put it on my Tribute CD. I recorded a Tribute CD of songs that Dad wrote, and I love to sing that song. It's got the greatest feeling to it. I get in the car and listen to the CD, and just the experience of recording it was such a great healing thing for me, because everyone who played on it was connected with Dad in some way, and they all loved him. They were all telling these stories, and talking and laughing... and I really needed that. It was a just a wonderful experience.

What other entertainers were you close to growing up? Who hung around your house?

The family friends were Jerry Kennedy and his bunch. He produced The Statler Brothers, Reba McEntire and Ray Stevens. Joe South was around when I was a little girl. Dad was from Atlanta and he and Ray Stevens were friends down there. They had a band and played together on weekends. I have baby movies of me learning how to walk with Ray Stevens and Joe and Daddy. But I was actually pretty protected and sheltered. I do remember Tammy Wynette a lot, though… she was a sweetheart. I love that woman. Boy, Daddy loved Faron Young, Chet Atkins, Glen Campbell, Bobby Bare, Brenda Lee… there were a bunch of them… I am trying to think of them.

In the story of *your* life, what memories do you have of holidays and special events with your father?

Christmas was the bomb in our family. Christmas was it. My favorite Christmas that I remember, I think I was like 10 years old and I had the mumps, or measles or something, and it was snowing. Back then we used to get lots of snow, and it was DEEP snow. And of course, all the family would come to spend the night at our house and celebrate… all the cousins and grandparents. And they'd say "You better go to bed, 'cause Santa Claus has gotta come!" One year, Daddy played Santa Claus, and I never had a clue. So we're in the house, and we hear this *thump thump thump* on the roof, and my grandmother played it up. "It's Santie Claus, look for him… do you see him?" We went running through the house, screaming and yelling and looking out the window. And then sure enough, here comes Santa walking across the yard and waving at us. He keeps walking, and you hear a *thump thump* on the roof. And then he's gone. That was best Christmas ever for me.

It turned out that Daddy had on the Santa suit, and he had big rocks that he was throwing on the roof so that we would think there were reindeer up there. So that was my favorite Christmas.

I love dogs and had a blonde Cocker Spaniel growing up. Please tell me about *your* pets, if any, or *your* pet as a child.

I had a dog named Elmo, but I was so little that I don't remember what kind of dog it was. Mama loved little bitty dogs, so we had Yorkshire Terriers and a little Pug at one time. My closest pet when I was a little girl was called FiFi, and she was a toy poodle. Then the last few years, Mom and Dad had a little toy poodle that looked like FiFi, and her name was Tinkerbelle. Daddy would not follow the rules... he was always sneaking and giving her peanut butter, and all these things. We had a Great Dane one time. He was a baby, but he was as big as a horse, and would run through the house. We had this marble floor in the foyer, and he'd run and hit the foyer and start sliding on his side. He ran into the living room one time and jumped on Daddy's lap in the recliner. The chair goes straight back with Daddy and the dog. I loved that dog. But Daddy loved animals. He wouldn't even kill a snake. One day there was a snake on the walkway and our neighbor came over with a shovel to kill it, but Daddy yelled "Don't kill it, he's just doing his thang!" The guy said "Reed... I am not going to ask him for his social security number." But Daddy didn't want him to kill it.

8

Explain to me how you were able to share *your* musical talents with your father. If not, how have you shared your talents with his fans?

Well, he was busy all the time when I was little. But I would sing along with his records, and I would sing along with Beatles albums, and beat on pots and pans. So Mama told Daddy I was singing and she got me to sing for him one day, and he said "Well, good for you." I was about 6 years old, and we went down into the basement. Back then, they had the flat top reel-to-reel recorders, and he recorded me singing the song "Feel For You", which is another song that I love. I put it on my Tribute Album as well. We always sang with family. When I was a kid, my relatives on my mother's side... there was always a boog-hoodle of relatives. We would go down to visit my grandmother, and everybody had a guitar, banjo, fiddle, mandolin or something, and we would all sing and play. At some point I started playing the piano, and one day when I was 14 or 15, he said "I want to take you to sing in this show with me at the Grand Ole

Opry." It was a benefit show for something, and that was my professional debut.

We would sing as a family on shows now and then. And then when I got older, he would take me on the road; but not all the time. I intended to have my own career, but I had a child about a decade earlier than I had planned on, and you couldn't pay me enough to leave that baby. I kept saying "I'm going to get the singing going", but I just couldn't do it… I couldn't leave that child. Now we do the Jerry Reed Tribute every year. And the guys who played with Dad, like Rick McClure, Bart Pike, Mike Wyatt, Mark Thornton… all these guys who worked with Dad and just loved him are like family to me, and I love these guys. And now I get to sing Daddy's music with them once a year. And they all played on my CD as well. Everyone was just so great. So I still get to enjoy that, and we all come together once a year. One of them said "We just leave the egos at the door and just love Jerry Reed for a couple of hours." So he left me a wonderful gift with all of that.

9

What do you miss most about your father?

I just miss *him*… his wit… just *him*. Home was a whole different world when daddy was there. I just miss the man that he was.

10

Do you have a website or Facebook page you would like to share?

I am in the process of getting a website, but you can purchase my Tribute CD on CDBaby.com. Type in Siedina Reed and the title is *"Today is Mine"* A Tribute To My Father Jerry Reed.

Facebook: Music page and personal page

WChrystie
ooley

1

The new Country Music Entertainers will leave a different kind of *Legacy* than your father had the opportunity to leave. How comfortable do you feel with today's Country Music?

I feel a lot like my father would have: that there's room for all kinds of music, as long as it's good music. I'm open-minded; however, do I personally love it? No. It doesn't make me feel the way that traditional Country music used to make me feel. It doesn't move me, personally. I miss the old Reba McEntire and the older stars that had

so much feeling behind their music. Today's music, to me, is just so commercial; it leaves me feeling very empty.

There are a few artists that I think are amazing, though. I think that Eric Church is really authentic and real, and I like him. I like what the Americana labels are doing. Music is gonna progress, and it's gonna change. There is no way that anything is going to stay exactly the same. I don't know how they could separate Jamey Johnson, Kacey Musgraves, and Chris Stapleton. Their music is authentic, but I don't think it holds a candle to the old Country music.

Sheb

2

As a child of a Country Music legend, what do you feel was the biggest event or experience that impacted *you* the most growing up?

Probably The Boys Club of America benefit show that my dad did every single year, because it was philanthropic, and he was helping people. My father would join forces with a black minister on Park Avenue, where my parents sent me to school. It was a very poor place, and it taught me not to be prejudiced. Prejudice is not in a person's DNA, and as a kid, you're not that way; you're taught it. My dad loved kids, and it was his way of giving back and trying to bring the communities together. So it was twofold. We also held benefits in Little Oakview, which was kinda like a little dust bowl community, and Soule Park and Oakview. It was, by and large, people from Bakersfield, Texas and Oklahoma, and people like that. Very blue-collar communities. Artists would come 'cause they were friends of my dad's and donate their time and talents to raise money. Paul Bringer, who played Wishbone on Rawhide,

emceed one year, and I got to meet him. Some of his best friends like Roger Miller, Buck Owens and his sons, and Merle always came. It was really cool to meet those people, bring the community together and help people who needed it.

3

Let's talk more about your life behind the curtain. So many of the Country singers were on the road most of the time. Share with me life at home with or without your father. How did that form your life's decisions and path?

I have a very big opinion on this one. When I look at every single kid whose parent was a music artist, especially in this era of our generation, it was very, very hard. Our parents weren't there, because they had to be on the road all the time. It was the only way that they made money. In the 80s era, some of the artists could actually stay home if they wrote songs, but it wasn't like that for us. Our parents were gone 24/7.

They didn't grow up with a silver spoon in their mouths, they grew up poor and had strong work ethics. They didn't know how to do anything except work hard, and work as hard as they could.

Some kids were lucky, and had a parent who was really family-oriented. I think that Jim Ed Brown would be a good example of that. I think he was really involved with his family, the best that he could be. But a lot of our parents were gone a lot. And then there was drug addiction, alcoholism mainly, and other things that came from not being home.

My parents never fought or talked to each other disrespectfully, but I can tell you that one of the biggest arguments my parents ever had was me going to my dad when he was home and asking him if I could do something. If I asked him and he said no, I would go and ask my mom and then she would say yes. So I would get to do it. My dad would be so ticked off and say, "Well, I don't even need to be here." And then my mom would defend me, saying, "Well, you're never here. Of course she's going to ask me, because I'm the one she always asks."

The truth is, my dad was a wonderful guy, and I knew that my dad loved me. But at the same time, I just remember when he came off the road, he still seemed like that public figure… no matter where we would go, he was still "on". And I think I can speak for a lot of the kids. You'd go out to dinner, and people were always coming up. Not just fans, but friends, coming up and talking to them. So you didn't get the family dinners like normal families who talk to each other. Then there was always someone pawing at them off the road who created issues. It made me want to have a normal life.

But according to my friends in college who had normal lives with parents who had jobs and were home every night, I didn't know how to have a normal life.

I got a regular job, and it looked good with some security, but I was bored out of my mind. I missed music and "my" life, so I left college and got a job as a backup singer with the Grand Ole Opry singers for six months. My life suddenly went back in the direction that I was most familiar with.

What single song was your favorite? Why?

Oh gosh, well, it had to be *"Only For You"*. I don't think it was even a single, but it meant a lot to me. Of course *"Purple People Eater"* was a fun song and everything, but it wasn't a song like *"Only For You"* that I wanted to listen to over and over again. He taught me the song, and we would sing it together... it was our time together. We actually sang it together in front of an audience after he taught it to me.

5

What other entertainers were you close to growing up? Who hung around your house?

Johnny Cash and Roger Miller, for sure. Those two were really tight with my dad. And Lisa Sutton's dad, Glen Sutton, was always up at the house, as well. My dad's best friend was Don Robertson; he was right up there with Roger. Don wrote "Please Help Me I'm Falling". He's in the Country Music Songwriter Hall of Fame. He was like my Godfather. He

and his wife Irene I'd say they were really, really close to my parents. Longevity would be Roger Miller, but then his life went in a different direction. My dad wasn't as racy as Roger. He was calmer than that. But Roger and Don and Glen and Johnny Cash... that's who I remember the most.

In the story of *your* life, what memories do you have of holidays and special events with your father?

Those memories are a little gloomy for me. I have a really good memory, just not good memories. It's kinda sad for me to talk about. I remember literally ONE Christmas. I remember the tree, and that I got a bridle for my horse. I don't remember any other Christmases with my parents. I know that we have to have done something for Christmas, or maybe not. I think things were different back then. Parents back then celebrated holidays differently. My life was very modest and humble; it wasn't the big, gift-giving thing that we do now.

I know I made a big deal out of every birthday with my kids. I made a really big deal out of Christmas. I tried to start traditions. Things that my kids remember even today, and I thank God that I did that. I even started a tradition that, on every Monday, because that was my day off, I'd buy them a little something that they'd been wanting. And I'd leave it on their floor with a card, so that when they got home from school they'd have it. I did that every single Monday.

7

I love dogs and had a blonde Cocker Spaniel growing up. Please tell me about *your* pets, if any, or *your* pet as a child.

I always had pets. That's probably the best memory. My dad had a dog named Smackdab, and it was a mutt. He had a black eye, and he was white. My dad LOVED that little dog. But that was my dad's dog, though. He had the biggest heart for animals. I had horses. Trixie was my first horse; she was a miniature paint. Paliodottie was my first really big horse. She was a racehorse. I actually entered a rodeo, western equitation event, and she was so used to the racetrack that when she saw those white fences, she tore out like she was on the racetrack. It was the funniest thing ever. After the event, the announcer said, "And she won, she won the race." Even when it was a walk, trot and canter event.

My first dog was a Collie, and I named it Apache. But it was shot by my neighbor in my front yard. I'm not kidding you! Then we had two cows, which I named Bluebell and Blackie. I'd get home from school every day and talk to them, and kiss on them. I loved those cows! One day I got home and started looking for them, and their hides were hanging over the fence. I had no idea that my dad was actually raising them for slaughter. I didn't talk to my dad for a long time, and consequently I was never a big meat eater after that. I do eat it now, but not often, and when I do, I do it reverently. But I always had a dog.

8

Explain to me how you were able to share *your* musical talents with your father. If not, how have you shared your talents with his fans?

Everything that I ever said I wanted to do after I got out of high school, he never approved of it. We sat down one day, and it was the only time I openly said that I wanted to be a flight attendant. And he said, "Oh, you don't want to do that. That's just a glorified waitress in the sky. You don't want to do that." Then I said, "Dad, I think I want to go to school and be a dental hygienist." And then he said, "No, you don't want to do that. You don't want to have your hands in people's mouths all day."

But when I told him that I wanted to sing... now that made him excited. Which was really weird, because he knew the downfalls. I was in a trio in school, and he knew my voice... So, for whatever reason, he believed in me, and he put his energy into trying to help me the best he could. I can remember him sitting down with me, and making me write a very realistic list of the pros and cons of the music industry, and the things that I would to be willing to sacrifice in order to make this happen. Some of those things weren't very appealing to me, and some were the very things that I didn't have, and wanted more than anything. Singing meant

putting off a family for the first five years, while you travel on the road and establish yourself first as an artist. When you're young, five years seems like your entire life, and that was hard for me. So I allowed him and my stepmother to manage my career. So then I wrote a song - and it was a pretty darn good song - with Don Robertson, and got a publishing deal with the Music Mill. Dad and I tried to write together, but I always ended up being his sounding board... he craved that kind of feedback. It was hard, working intimately with your parent.

I was able to share a lot of stories and his music with his fans on the Country's Family Reunion "Second Generations" DVD series by Larry Black.

What do you miss most about your father?

Well... I missed him a lot before he was gone. He chose these real screwball wives after he and my mom split. I was 14 when my parents decided to separate. I remember, very specifically, them sitting down with me and telling me that they were going to separate. And they handled it very well. I said "It's fine with me, as long as you're still my dad and you'll still be here." But that didn't really happen. He kept having relationships that weren't really healthy, and because of them, it kept me further from him and the relationship that every kid needs with a parent.

But I do I miss his big, strong, powerful presence. And he was funny. I do miss his sense of humor. He just had charisma, and he also had a deep spiritual side to him. He was a very mindful, introspective person, which most people wouldn't think he would be, because he was a comedian. He meditated an hour every single morning, and he took the time out to refocus his energy and his thoughts, because he struggled all the time with his humanness. That part of him, I absolutely adored. Very, very, real.

Do you have a website or Facebook page you would like to share?

I only have a personal Facebook page.

Lisa Anderson

1

The new Country Music Entertainers will leave a different kind of *Legacy* than your mother had the opportunity to leave. How comfortable do you feel with today's Country Music?

I am fine with it. You know, I hear a lot of rumblings, of course. "Oh, it ain't the old Country." My grandfather in particular, he's got a lot of Merle Haggard stuff, even before mom. He just thinks that all this new stuff is not the same. Now, I do understand that it ain't gonna leave the same legacy, unless you are a Carrie Underwood. It does seem like sons and daughters of singers become singers themselves. But I don't have a problem with the new Country; I think it leads into a couple of different genres now. For example, you've got Americana that's kinda absorbing a lot of the classic Country. There are still guys who are kicking butt on that sound. Chris Stapleton has got that sound, but then you've also got your Luke Bryans and your Jason Aldeans. It's kinda like Pop, Electronica, Heavy Metal… you know, it's just that Country has some different varies now, and I think it just opens it up more for all of us.

Lynn

2

As a child of a Country Music legend, what do you feel was the biggest event or experience that impacted *you* the most growing up?

I have no idea. So much of it was the whole body of the childhood. You know I was lucky.... Losing mom recently and having lost dad, looking back now I just don't know what event, and even at the time, I didn't realize what was really important. But boy, I got to do a lot of things, and so did my parents. There were award shows, and horse shows, and then holidays. I don't know just one single thing or a good answer.

3

Let's talk more about *your* life behind the curtain. So many of the Country singers were on the road most of the time. Share with me life at home with or without your mother. How did that form your life's decisions and path?

Ah... I don't know about the life decisions and paths, 'cause I certainly didn't go down some of the same roads that my mom did. Mom was on the road a lot when I was really young, and mom and dad didn't divorce until I was seven. They'd been married for ten years, and so up until seven I was with my dad or grandparents. Later on, I remember a lot of airports and stuff, but then I'd go back home and ride horses. I told a reporter one time that Mom, whether at a recording studio or at a horse show or at home... she was just Mom to me.

And I was always with them, either mom or my dad or my grandparents, I was always around.

What single song was your favorite? Why?

"Keep Me In Mind", I guess because my dad wrote it. I just love that song and the way that my mom sings it. And I love the way that it was recorded.

What other entertainers were you close to growing up? Who hung around your house?

We had more songwriters around than entertainers. Mom was always into songwriters, and I don't know if it was because she grew up with Granny and Grandpa, who were also songwriters. And she married my dad, who was a songwriter. For the last thirty years, she has been with Mentor Williams, and he's a songwriter. During my formative years, it was always songwriters like Larry Henley, Billy Brunette and Dennis Morgan hanging out at the house.

6

In the story of *your* life, what memories do you have of holidays and special events with your mother?

Our holidays were all over the place, so I don't know about that one.

7

I love dogs and had a blonde Cocker Spaniel growing up. Please tell me about *your* pets, if any, or *your* pet as a child.

We always had horses and dogs. My big pet as a kid with mom was an Australian Shepherd. We always had Aussie's. She had Aussies until the day she died. *Kansas* was a puppy that somebody had given her onstage at a show at a state fair in Kansas. I was probably 4 or 5, and she brought that puppy home on the bus. We had her until she died, about twenty years later. She had gone through several different marriages and more kids being added to the family, and I loved Kansas. We also had a bunch of great horses. *Bett High* … Mom gave her to me. I begged and begged for about four years, and it was the best horse ever. It was real athletic and good, and kinda made me become a good rider. And then *Bett* and I went and kicked butt at a lot of horse shows and championships. That was the same horse that mom broke; so, thanks to her, I got to ride a good one. When she retired, she was put out at my trainer's farm, and I got to go see her in her old age. But now she is buried there, out behind the swimming pool.

8

Explain to me how you were able to share *your* musical talents with your mother. If not, how have you shared your talents with her fans?

I don't have any musical talents. My talents have been on the business side of things. For sixteen years, I have been manufacturing CDs and doing graphic design for album covers. Throughout the years, here and there she and a fan would have a record coming up, and I would put it together. Now recently, I did the new *Bridges* record with her. But since her passing, sharing with the fans has been interesting lately. That's a new arena there. Dad didn't have fans when he passed -he just had a lot of Nashville Music Row buddies and a lot of great songs. But with mom, I posted something for Mother's Day, and it had over 100,000 likes. I have been keeping things and putting them on Facebook, and letting fans purchase them. I am saving the money, and I just ordered Lynn Anderson Yellow Roses for next year. We will be selling them in 2017 and donating the money to different charities mom supported.

9

What do you miss most about your mother?

I think her energy. She was going a mile a minute. Every day, she was always thinking up something to do.

10

Do you have a website or Facebook page you would like to share?

www.facebook.com/ SideStreet Sutton

www.facebook.com/ OfficialLynn Anderson

George Hamilton V

1

The new Country Music Entertainers will leave a different kind of *Legacy* than your father had the opportunity to leave. How comfortable do you feel with today's Country Music?

From the mid-1960s onward, my Dad's music was called "Folk-Country": a forerunner to what is now called "Americana" Music. I never really listened to a lot of Country Music on the radio, other than what I'd heard growing up at the Opry, back in the Ryman Auditorium days (the Country Music made by the parents of my group of "Second Generation" kids).

I don't hear a lot of today's Country music, but I probably feel more comfortable with today's Americana Music.

2

As a child of a Country Music legend, what do you feel was the biggest event or experience that impacted *you* the most growing up?

The biggest experience that impacted me growing up was definitely performing as

George

"George Hamilton IV & V" with my Dad on the Grand Ole Opry for twenty-eight years. The dynamic that I had with my father was not only "father and son", but also "vocal duo" and "touring partners" for many years. So my story might be a bit different from that of most other "Second Generation" kids.

3

Let's talk more about your life behind the curtain. So many of the Country singers were on the road most of the time. Share with me life at home with or without your father. How did that form your life's decisions and path?

My Dad taught me three chords on the guitar at the kitchen table one morning, in between his travels around the world. Billboard Magazine gave Dad the title "The International Ambassador of Country Music" in the 1970s, for all of his international tours, television shows, and recordings. He was the first to take Country Music "Behind the Iron Curtain" in March of 1974, which included several sold out arena concerts in Czechoslovakia.

The stories that he brought home with him from his world travels were legendary! As a professional singer-songwriter when I became trapped in the Nashville "cookie-cutter cowboy factory" in the 1990s, I remembered my Dad's stories about there being a world of Country Music fans OUTSIDE of America. My Dad made a highly successful music career for himself overseas, and so that's why I decided to do the same.

I'm mighty glad that I followed dad's Inspiration! I've been enjoying my music career overseas since 1990. I recently returned from a cross-country theatre tour of Scotland, and I'll be in Poland this Summer. Then I've got a nationwide theatre tour of England next Spring, and a cross-country tour in Scotland again later in the year!

4

What single song was your favorite? Why?

I can't really limit my favorite to a single song. I LOVE 'em all, and I LOVE singing 'em all!

5

What other entertainers were you close to growing up? Who hung around your house?

I only lived in Nashville from 1960 through around 1972 (twelve years). Then we moved to North Carolina, where my Mom and Dad were originally from, so that we'd be closer to family while my Dad was spending a lot of time outside the country, hosting his Canadian TV Series and BBC-TV Series throughout the 1970s and early '80s. At the same time, my Dad became partners with Arthur "Guitar Boogie" Smith (who also wrote "Duelin' Banjos") in a TV Show that was filmed in Charlotte, NC and syndicated across America. Later, I went to the University of North Carolina at Chapel Hill (my Dad's Alma Mater). So we weren't in Nashville during my teen years onward, where most of my memories seem to begin.

But from my twelve childhood Nashville years, I remember my family going on picnics with Shelly West and her Mom Dottie. Robyn Young played football with us and our neighbors in our front yard, on Fredericksburg Drive.

Our family was really close with the Bill Anderson Family. Bill's Daughter Teri and I used to sing songs together, while she played on her Mom's piano. Rumor has it that Teri was even my first girlfriend! Our family was also really close with the John D. Loudermilk Family. My Dad and John D. started their musical careers together back in North Carolina in the 1950s. And my brother Peyton, and I were around the same age as the three Loudermilk sons, so we all spent a lot of time together; we were even babysat by the Allman Brothers (then called the "Allman Joys") when John D. was producing them (Legend has it that "George IV" and "John D." discovered the Allman Brothers in Nashville, back in the 1960s. John D. originally wrote "Break My Mind" for the Allman Brothers, but George IV ended-up having the hit record with it). Gordon Lightfoot was our houseguest back in the 1960s, when he came down to Nashville to record his guitar on George IV's recording of Gordon's "Steel Rail Blues". I've heard stories of a lot of Nashville Artists coming to meet Gordon Lightfoot at our house on Fredericksburg Drive during his visit.

In the story of *your* life, what memories do you have of holidays and special events with your father?

My Dad was always home for Christmas! Many of my holiday memories of my Father include family gatherings at our house, or with relatives. But for twenty-eight of my "professional" years, singing together on the Opry at Christmastime was always special, especially at the Ryman Auditorium! One year, my son ("George VI") and my sister (Mary) joined Dad and me in singing "Silent Night" on the Opry. Dad also performed a mesmerizing version of "The Christmas Guest", in tribute to Grandpa Jones. The Opry audiences were so hypnotized by George IV's rendition, you could've heard a pin drop!

My most recent memory of George IV and Christmas is from 2013, when he gave his "Christmas in The Country" program as a special presentation of my "Viva! NashVegas® Radio Show" out here at the hardware store in Downtown Franklin, Tennessee, which is where we did the radio show at the time. You can watch George IV and his "Christmas Stories, Songs & Candle Light Carols" program on my YouTube site: www.NashVegas.TV, and via this direct link: https://www.youtube.com/watch?v=X5RYK1kHdm0

I love dogs and had a blonde Cocker Spaniel growing up. Please tell me about *your* pets, if any, or *your* pet as a child.

We've currently got three cats, a dog, and a parrot that flies around our house. A raccoon and a possum also drop by every night to feast on the cats' food on our back porch. When I was growing up, we had a Collie named Chester, after my Dad's close friend and producer, Chester B. Atkins (aka "Chet"). We also had a Siamese cat that John D. Loudermilk saw as a kitten and said "Man, that cat is too much!" So my parents named the cat "Too Much".

8

Explain to me how you were able to share *your* musical talents with your father. If not, how have you shared your talents with his fans?

My Dad and I performed together as "George Hamilton IV & V" on the Opry for twenty-eight years. We also performed concerts and at international festivals together, when our solo international touring schedules allowed. We headlined concerts and festivals together in America, Canada, Japan, England, Scotland, Ireland, France, the Czech Republic, Germany, Poland, and even Lithuania! We recorded four studio albums together as "George Hamilton IV & George Hamilton V"!

My Dad also recorded my song "We Will Meet Again" on several of his albums. I'm mighty proud that he loved that song so much! And one of his recordings of the song was even with the legendary Skeeter Davis! We also performed the song at the Grand Ole Opry with Skeeter many times. George IV and I sang "We Will Meet Again" on the "Country's Family Reunion Second Generations" episode. We also co-hosted two episodes of our "HomeGrown Radio Hour" on WSM-650 Radio, where we shared career stories and our favorite recordings by our favorite artists.

George IV also participated in several episodes of my "Viva! NashVegas® Radio Show". If you have the chance, go to www.NashVegas.TV and search for "George Hamilton IV on the Viva Nashvegas Radio Show". You'll find George IV "Co-Starring" on the episodes with special guests Bill Anderson, John D. Loudermilk, and Lynn Anderson. I'm also mighty glad that we had the chance to celebrate George IV's 54th Anniversary with the Grand Ole Opry on the "Viva! NashVegas® Radio Show" in February 2014! Brenda Lee and State Senator Jack Johnson were all special guests on the Feb. 8, 2014 episode.

9

What do you miss most about your father?

I have audio recordings of my Dad telling the story of his life and music career. I interviewed him for the Harper-Collins biography "George Hamilton IV - Ambassador of Country Music". So I listen to those interviews from time to time, to hear him talking. We've also got tons of video from when Dad and I were on TV shows like "Nashville Now", "Opry LIVE", and of course "Country's Family Reunion" and my "Viva! NashVegas® Radio Show". So I also watch those videos from time to time to see him "in motion", as well. I can even see and hear us "in motion", performing together.

Two things I miss the most:

1. Actually singing LIVE with my Dad. You can't beat the family harmony, interaction and connection.

2. The handshakes and hugs that we'd trade at the end of our Opry spots, as the curtain was coming down. Our last handshake and hug was on Sept. 6, 2014, at the end of our final Opry Spot. We closed with one of Dad's favorite songs that we sang together: *"Forever Young"*.

10

Do you have a website or Facebook page you would like to share?

My Facebook Pages:

www.Facebook.com/ VivaNash VegasRadioShow

www.Facebook.com/ George HamiltonV

www.Facebook.com/ FolksyFest

www.Facebook.com/ VivaNashVegas

My Website: www.VivaNash Vegas.com

My YouTube Channel: www. Nash Vegas.TV

Photos courtesy of: Heart of Texas Records, Kyoto Japan, and Gillian Keating

Becky *Ashworth*

1

The new Country Music Entertainers will leave a different kind of *Legacy* than your father had the opportunity to leave. How comfortable do you feel with today's Country Music?

The Country Music Industry is so totally different from back in the 60s and 70s. But that is to be expected, because that is progress. I think that some of the entertainers of today's Country Music will be considered great artists, like Garth Brooks, Alan Jackson, Brad Paisley, Blake Shelton, Reba McEntire, Carrie Underwood and Miranda Lambert.

2

As a child of a Country Music legend, what do you feel was the biggest event or experience that impacted *you* the most growing up?

Being able to experience the backstage at the Opry, and getting to meet the artists, knowing that they all loved what they were doing.

3

Let's talk more about your life behind the curtain. So many of the Country singers were on the road most of the time. Share with me life at home with or without your father. How did that form your life's decisions and path?

Ernie

Daddy started being on the road when I was 12, so it was a normal way of life for us. Any time that school was out, we traveled with Daddy. It was a great experience, to see so much of the United States, and we would always stop at any radio stations on the way so that Daddy could go in with his record and talk with the DJ. Some things that I'd read about in school, I was now seeing firsthand. It made me appreciate how hard being on the road really was, not only for Daddy, but for Mama too. I guess that is why I chose a career that did not involve traveling.

What single song was your favorite? Why?

"I Wish". That is my favorite song that Daddy did. The song dealt with such yearning from someone so in love. "I wish that I could be your coat, your hat, your shoes, then I know that sometimes I would be close to you." Who hasn't felt like this?

What other entertainers were you close to growing up? Who hung around your house?

I can remember a lot of the Opry members coming to the house. Bob Luman, Jim Ed Brown, Charlie Louvin, The 4 Guys, Jean Shepard, Dottie West, Roy Acuff... sometimes it looked like you were backstage at the Opry, with all the people who came by.

6

In the story of *your* life, what memories do you have of holidays and special events with your father?

I will never forget my 16th birthday. It fell on a Saturday, and Daddy took me to the Opry with him. He gave me an Opry Book, told everyone that it was my 16th birthday and then had everyone sign the book. When it was his turn on stage, he called me up, announced to everyone that it was my birthday, and then all the entertainers came up on stage and sang *"Happy Birthday"*. I so wish that we would have had a video camera with us, to capture this extraordinary moment.

I love dogs and had a blonde Cocker Spaniel growing up. Please tell me about *your* pets, if any, or *your* pet as a child.

We had always had cats until Daddy was booked in Seattle, and then for some reason, he brought home a Toy Poodle, and he named him Haffy. That dog loved my Mother; he was her protector. We had Haffy for twenty years. When Haffy died, Mama and Daddy bought a plot in a pet cemetery for him.

8

Explain to me how you were able to share *your* musical talents with your father. If not, how have you shared your talents with his fans?

Unfortunately, I do not have any musical talent. I cannot carry a tune in a bucket. What I did get talent-wise from Daddy was the ability to write poems. I worked for Daddy at his radio station in Ardmore, Tennessee - and when he wanted to sell

it, I bought it. I have been able to satisfy my love of music by programming a radio station. That is also how I have kept his music out there, for new and old fans.

What do you miss most about your father?

I miss Daddy's sense of humor and his ability to make everything seem better. No matter how serious the circumstances, he always stood by me and things didn't seem so bad.

10

Do you have a website or Facebook page you would like to share?

The station has a website: Wslvam1110.com, and a Facebook page: WSLV am 1110.

I just want to say that I would not trade my life growing up for anything. It was a completely different way of life than any of my friends had. I have seen and experienced things that are truly remarkable.

Hawkshaw
awkins Jr

1

The new Country Music Entertainers will leave a different kind of *Legacy* than your father had the opportunity to leave. How comfortable do you feel with today's Country Music?

Well… okay, here's kinda the way that I look at that: I don't think that today's Country is yesterday's Country. I'm not knocking what they're doing these days, 'cause I like it, but they should give them their own *genre*; don't call it *Country*. Country should have its own special place on the Billboard charts, along with whatever it is they're doing. I'm not mad at anybody for taking Country music in that direction… I just get tired of hearing about girls in shorts drinking beer on the back of trucks.

2

As a child of two Country Music legends, what do you feel was the biggest event or experience that impacted *you* the most growing up?

Well, it happened after I was already "grown up". It was when they put Mama into the *Hall of Fame*. That was such a precious night. We had gotten the red carpet treatment, and as

Hawkshaw

I was getting back into the limo after Mama got inducted, she looked up, and it said *Country Music Hall of Fame* - and I wish that I had had a camera. Tears were rolling down her cheeks, and she looked at her husband Benny and said, "Well dad, I guess we have come about as far as we could go." I broke down and started crying like a baby. It tore me up. And that was definitely the biggest moment for me in my parents' history.

Let's talk more about your life behind the curtain. So many of the Country singers were on the road most of the time. Share with me life at home with or without your parents. How did that form your life's decisions and path?

It did… you know, with both of them being entertainers, they both had to be out on the road. Of course, Hawk died a month before I was born. So Mama brought in Kay Helfrich to help. I called her "*other mama*", and she stayed with us and practically raised us while Mama was out on the road. Mama would come home every

other month or so and shower us with gifts, so we were spoiled rotten little brats. But Kay helped Mama raise us. She was from Fort Wayne, Indiana, and I love her very much.

What single song was your favorite? Why?

I like the tempo and melody of "*Twenty Miles From Shore*". That's my favorite one of his to sing. But my favorite song that Hawk sang is "*If I Ever Get Rich, Mom*". I will never match the level of success that my mother achieved, but I've always dreamed of having her "a *pathway of roses in place of cold stone*". And that's the line in the song that I felt like he was singing to my grandma, you know.

Of course, "*Lonesome 77203*" is the one paying the bills.

5

What other entertainers were you close to growing up? Who hung around your house?

Bill Anderson, George Morgan... I mean, I have been so truly blessed to have met so many of them and to have hung out with them, eaten finger sandwiches with them. Mostly, I would say Bill Anderson was probably my mama's biggest advocate at the time. When he was a DJ, my mother was his first interview. When he came to town and started writing songs, mama did an entire Bill Anderson album. And he's such a great writer. I remember Bill coming over once, and he had brought the original copy in a frame of *"Slippin' Away"*, and gave that to my mom. Back in the day when I was about 5, 6 or 7 years old, I remember that Jackie Phelps and the musicians from the Opry would come over to our house. We had a nice house, and a big room where they would all just sit down and play bluegrass music, and you could tell that it was nothing but just fun for them.

6

In the story of *your* life, what memories do you have of holidays and special events?

Well, I know that every Thanksgiving and every Christmas, of course, everybody meets at Mama's house. Mama makes the big meal. So all of my holidays are pretty much centered around Mama. Now... during the summertime when Mama would travel on the bus, my brother Donnie and I would get to go with her. She was playing all of these state parks, and all of these fairs and stuff. Well, because we were who we were, they would have someone to watch after us. They would take us to ride the Roller Coaster and Ferris Wheel, to eat cotton candy... things like that. That is what I remember the most.

7

I love dogs and had a blonde Cocker Spaniel growing up. Please tell me about *your* pets, if any, or *your* pet as a child.

Oh gosh... Freckles was my dog. She was half German Shepherd and half Collie. Every night, and especially on Sundays, we would watch the Walt Disney show, and Freckles would come up and lay down, and she would be my pillow right in front of the TV. This was back when we only had four channels. But Freckles would be my pillow for hours. Then Freckles got ran over and it broke her tailbone. Mama left me the option to either have her put down, or to have her tail cut off, and she would then have to go through a couple of surgeries. But I just couldn't lose Freckles, so I opted to have her without a tail. It made her look kind of funny, but that was my dog, and that will always be my dog.

Explain to me how you are able to share *your* musical talents and the music of your father?

Well, I do as many shows as possible, and I try and do my best when I'm doing their songs. I am a writer, so I do a lot of my stuff at shows, but I always pay homage to mom and dad. I do go by Hawk, but my legal name is Harold Franklin Hawkins II - not Jr. I run dad's Facebook page, and I run Mama's Facebook page, but I am actually not too adept on the computer. Mama's is

off the chain. It gets about 300 *likes* a day. It's crazy. I try to respond to everyone that I can, but it's overwhelming, especially on her page.

9

What is one of your favorite stories about your father?

I've heard so many, but now the one that sticks out the most is by one of my dad's friends, Harlan Howard. Harlan told me this story, and I probably shouldn't say this, 'cause I really don't want this out. But I guess that Hawk had a little girlfriend on the side or something... and I'm not sure if they were married yet, but I know that Harlan saw my mama pull up once, and knew that Hawk was up in the building with this girl. So Harlan made a mad jog to the green room, or wherever they were, and told my daddy that Jean was here.

You know, I used to write for Harlan. I was one of the few people who got to write for him. He would call me Kid... *"Come here Kid!"* Every day he would meet me down at the bar, - I think he drank Vodka and Cranberry - and he would say "*Come up here, kid, and let me buy you lunch.*" He was a great, great man, and a dear friend.

Do you have a website or Facebook page you would like to share?

Facebook.com/Hawkshaw-hawkins-jr

JeanShepardcountry.com

Kathy Louvin

1

The new Country Music Entertainers will leave a different kind of *Legacy* than your father had the opportunity to leave. How comfortable do you feel with today's Country Music?

I am a traditionalist. Dyed in the wool, hillbilly-loving Country Music brat. When Dad and Uncle Charlie did their thing, that's what it was: their thing. It wasn't a contest. They weren't trying to copy anyone, they had their favorites as everyone does... but it was about the gift that they had, and the passion it took to drive it from a farm on Sand Mountain, Alabama all the way to the stages of the world.

2

As a child of a Country Music legend, what do you feel was the biggest event or experience that impacted *you* the most growing up?

I think when Patsy and Hawk and those folks went down in the plane, at that point I sort of put on my big girl pants and realized, with horrific clarity, that the next time Daddy went out on the road, he may not come back alive. I was at my Aunt Kitty's [Smiley and Kitty Wilson].

Ira

Uncle Smiley booked Hawk, Loretta and Jean Shepard. So we were anticipating the arrival of that flight, only to get that awful phone call that left us all screaming and crying.

Let's talk more about your life behind the curtain. So many of the Country singers were on the road most of the time. Share with me life at home with or without your father. How did that form your life's decisions and path?

Most of the time, when they'd go out on the road, I'd stay at my Daddy's parents' farm, and I loved every minute of it. I'd hide in the mountains when they'd come to get me; I didn't ever want to leave the mountain. Other times, I had a nanny whom I loved almost as much as my grandmother. Everyone called her my "black mama". Her name was Manilla, and she was an angel. I never wanted to be in the music business. I swore I never would. And I held out until I turned 30.

What single song was your favorite? Why?

"When I Stop Dreaming". It was the one, the first secular song that the Louvins had ever done, and they'd been told by Capitol that if they flopped as a secular act, they'd lose their contract, period. It didn't flop.

What other entertainers were you close to growing up? Who hung around your house?

Bill Monroe, Patsy Cline, Loretta, Buddy Emmons, Shot Jackson, Melba Montgomery, George Jones, Joe and Rose Lee Maphis, Lightin' Chance, Martha Carson, etc.

In the story of *your* life, what memories do you have of holidays and special events with your father?

I don't have a treasure trove of good memories with my parents. There was torment and turmoil in our home most of the time. I have trouble with holidays even now, because the memories are very painful.

7

I love dogs and had a blonde Cocker Spaniel growing up. Please tell me about *your* pets, if any, or *your* pet as a child.

The most favorite pet of ours was a Cockapoo named Noodle-O.

8

Explain to me how you were able to share *your* musical talents with your father. If not, how have you shared your talents with his fans?

I've been singing for as long as I can remember. Sometimes, during one of the famous "jam sessions", they'd get me up in the middle of the night, or morning, to sing. I didn't get to share any of my success with either of them, as they both passed in their early 40s, but I have been blessed with a 30-year award-winning career as a singer-songwriter, and I recently accepted the Lifetime Achievement Award from the Grammy Association on my Dad's behalf.

9

What do you miss most about your father?

What I miss most about Dad is the music. What I miss most about Mom is her presence.

10

Do you have a website or Facebook page you would like to share?

www.louvin.rocks

Georgette Jones

1

The new Country Music Entertainers will leave a different kind of *Legacy* than your parents had the opportunity to leave. How comfortable do you feel with today's Country Music?

To be fair, I think that there definitely are some really talented artists out there today. Unfortunately, I feel it's been dictated differently now by a business, and all it's about the money. It isn't artistry and creativity as much as it used to be, so I do think that does change it. I believe that a lot of people who may have had the opportunity to make good music are left behind and ignored, because they don't fit a certain image. That's the only thing that I really hate about today. If we had missed out on the artists from the past simply because they didn't look the part, then gosh, we would have really lost a lot of incredible music. I am hoping that maybe that will shift… and I think it is starting to shift a little bit with artists like Chris Stapleton, and Mo Pitney especially… they are amazing. Both of them have incredible talent. So I am hoping that people realize they are missing out on some wonderful music and lyrics that matter and mean something.

George & Tammy

2

As a child of two Country Music legends, what do you feel was the biggest event or experience that impacted *you* the most growing up?

Well, I think when I was little, I really never looked at my parents the way that other people did; they were just mom and dad to me. I guess I was in my early 20s before it really, finally hit me as to what kind of impact my parents' music and what they did , and how it influenced other people. In fact, I specifically remember even after my mom had gone and done the Rainforest Benefit with Sting, Elton John, Whitney Houston and several other people. At that time, I was young and was a big fan Whitney Houston and Elton John, and she came home and there was a Rolling Stone article about the event; I was reading it while she was making us biscuits and gravy in the kitchen. And mom was a whole centerfold of the Rolling Stone magazine, on like 4 or 5 pages, a huge spread... and it basically stated that the only standing ovation of the entire night came when mom sang *"Stand By Your Man"*. And I

think at that moment, it kinda really hit me. Oh my gosh, with all of those other people there, and as famous as those other people are, and with all the different genres of music that were there... that mom was the one that people stood up for. I was just amazed with that. And there have been other things like that with my dad as well. You just don't think about them like that until you get older. I am so appreciative of my parents for so many reasons, but I'm just now, as I get older, appreciating their music in the way that I should.

3

Let's talk more about your life behind the curtain. So many of the Country singers were on the road most of the time. Share with me life at home with or without either one of your parents or both. How did that form your life's decisions and path?

I grew up more with mom than I did with dad, but them both being gone a lot certainly impacted me, in such a way that when I got old enough to make a choice on what I wanted to do with my own life, I loved music, and it was certainly a passion for me as well... but I wanted to be at home, and I wanted a family, and I wanted to have children. I felt like, as much as I love my parents - and I certainly didn't hold it against them - I wanted to be at home. So I was a registered nurse for seventeen years before I finally decided to branch out and start doing music. I waited until my children got older. But I think that, the way we grew up, you really appreciate so much more than people often think you appreciate. It's not so much about the glamorous lifestyle; it's about the time with your family and who's important to you, and making memories with them. So mom especially made sure that when she was home, even if we had limited time, she wanted to make sure we had quality time together. Mom died when I was only 27 years old, and at that moment I realized that we are not guaranteed a single second. It was really important to me then to make relationships the main priority in my life and nothing else.

What single songs were your favorite? Why?

Of mom and dad together, I loved *"Take Me"*. That's one of my favorite songs that they ever did. It's not one of their more popular ones, but I just thought the way that they both sang it, along with the words to it, were beautiful. But I also loved *"Near You"*.

As for one on her own, I always say that it's the two -til songs, *"Til I Can Make It On My Own"* and *"Til I Make It Right"*. And it may have been 'cause I could relate a lot to it growing up. My dad... I always loved *"The Corvette Song"* as the fun song, but *"Walk Through This World With Me"* is probably one of my favorites out of my dad's slower songs. There were so many to pick from, but those were definitely my favorites.

What other entertainers were you close to growing up? Who hung around your house?

Loretta Lynn was a very close friend to my mom, and

Jan Howard was also very close to my mom. I saw them quite often. Many times, either Waylon and Jesse or Johnny and June would be at the house. Plenty of times, they would all come over and visit, and they'd hang out with both mom and dad at different times. They all remained friends, even after mom and dad divorced. And it was kinda strange, 'cause I didn't think about it so much when I was younger, but as I became an adult I didn't see them around as much. I didn't really appreciate the fact that I could have paid more attention to what was going on around me. When you're a kid, you just think *"Ah, those are just mom and dads' friends"*, and you're just playing and doing your own thing. I do look back now and think that I have some wonderful memories of being around some incredibly talented and wonderful people.

—— 6 ——

In the story of *your* life, what memories do you have of holidays and special events with your parents?

Holidays were always a big family get-together. Christmas was especially a really big, important holiday for us. Mom went all out. The whole month was *Christmas Crazy*. And I also have wonderful memories of Christmas with my Dad. But I do have to tell you about one particular Thanksgiving. I hate to share more memories of my mother, but I did grow up more with my mom than my dad. There were only one or two times that she had been away and we didn't have Thanksgiving together. However, when I got married to my children's father, we were living in Alabama and were spending that Thanksgiving with my husband's family. And mom knew that I was a little depressed, 'cause she always made a big 3-4 day event out of Thanksgiving, and I hated not being there. About three days before Thanksgiving, I got this enormous - and I mean HUGE - styrofoam box, and inside everything was packed on dry ice. Mom had sent everything that she normally made for Thanksgiving and mailed it to us! Biscuits for breakfast… desserts… everything that you could possibly imagine for a Thanksgiving meal. And it wasn't just enough for one day, but enough food frozen for me and my husband to eat for two or three weeks. Just to have meals from Mom's house was so very thoughtful and special.

7

I love dogs and had a blonde Cocker Spaniel growing up. Please tell me about *your* pets, if any, or *your* pet as a child.

We always had pets. We were heartbroken if we saw a stray, and we never passed on taking them home. So we had multiple cats and dogs at our house all the time. We even had a brown skunk that mom brought home one day. Her name was Ms. Pew.

My husband and I have three cats. One is named after Vince Gill (his name is Vince) and one is named after Paul Franklin - my husband is a steel guitar player - so, Franklin. And the newest cat is named Abbey.

We love dogs too, but unfortunately we travel so much, and of course they need more maintenance than a cat. But maybe one day we will be able to have a dog too.

8

Explain to me how you were able to share *your* musical talents with your parents. If not, how have you shared your talents with their fans?

I grew up singing with both my mom and my dad. I started singing when I was 3 years old. Mom would always encourage us to come out and sing when we were on the road with her, and any time that I saw my dad, he would do the same thing. I'd sing a couple of songs on my own, and then I would sing a duet with him, which was very special. It made me feel special, being a part of his music and sharing it with him. They both taught me an awful lot, and I like to sing their music when I do shows, 'cause I want people to always remember them and their music, and I like to honor them in that way. But I also write and do some of my own music as well. Hopefully the fans will like that too.

9

What do you miss most about your mother and your father?

Gosh, that's a very difficult one.

Just hearing their voice and getting a hug from either one of them would be the most amazing thing ever. Sorry... I am trying not to get emotional, but it's been a difficult week. This is the anniversary of my mom's death. And dad passed away on April 26th. There are too many things to mention that I miss. I miss them every day. You think you're okay. You can talk about music, and talk about events, but when you get down and talk about *them*... I miss them both.

10

Do you have a website or Facebook page you would like to share?

Facebook page: Georgette jonesmusic

Twitter: Georgettejonesmusic

Website: Georegettjones.net

Jesse Whitley

1

The new Country Music Entertainers will leave a different kind of *Legacy* than your father had the opportunity to leave. How comfortable do you feel with today's Country Music?

You know, there is definitely some stuff out there that I like a lot, but I feel like some of the stuff being played on *"Country Radio"* now is not Country music. It might be "good" music, but it's not Country. I think some of the people who call themselves Country artists now are actually Pop artists. That's just my opinion.

2

As a child of two Country Music legends, what do you feel was the biggest event or experience that impacted *you* the most growing up?

You know, that would probably be playing my Opry debut at the Ryman Auditorium two years ago. It was a Country Classic Show, and I was a part of it. It also happened to be May 9th... the 25th Anniversary of my father being gone. So it was bittersweet.

Keith

3

Let's talk more about your life behind the curtain. So many of the Country singers were on the road most of the time. Share with me life at home with or without your parents. How did that form your life's decisions and path?

I have been on the road a lot... along with my mom. I was more on the road than I was really at home a lot. It kinda helped me to grow up a little bit faster. There were a lot of times where I had to do things on my own. Most kids would say "Hey dad, can you help with this?" or "Can somebody take me here?" We didn't have that. But my mom did a great job. Being on the road helped me learn how to make my own dreams come true, and allowed me to do what I wanted to do for my whole life. It really showed me the "ins" and "outs" of this business, and it has been a real lesson-learner. I also learned how to handle things professionally.

4

What single song of your father's is your favorite? Why?

"I'm Losing You All Over Again"... it's hard... I'm just going to say *"I'm Losing You All Over Again"*... that's it.

5

What other entertainers were you close to growing up? Who hung around your house?

When I was growing up, Shelby Lynn and Kelly Lang would come around, but once I started getting older, I became friends with a lot of these singers and formed good friendships with them... Daryl Worley, Andy Griggs, Kevin Denny... now I have lifelong friendships with these guys. It's fun, 'cause they are really awesome and great people, and they have taught me a lot.

6

In the story of *your* life, what memories do you have of holidays or special events?

During the holidays, my mom always made it a point to be home. She gave us the best Christmases that we could ever have, and our families were always together during the holidays… always. It was great. My mom had a song called *"Christmas At Our House",* and ever since she wrote that song, Christmas is never Christmas until I hear that song playing, because it takes me back to when I was a kid and had nothing to worry about. Santa was there, and the magic was real.

7

I love dogs and had a blonde Cocker Spaniel growing up. Please tell me about *your* pets, if any, you had as a child.

We had dogs, dogs and dogs. We had an African Gray Bird that used to like to talk, and they live a long time. But I just love dogs, and it took me a long time to learn just how much dogs love people and how much people love dogs. That was really when I became a huge dog lover, and I really do love dogs… they are my favorite.

8

Explain how you are able to share *your* musical talents with your dad and mother's fans.

You know, being out here on the road with my mom, I get the chance to go out and play a couple songs during a show here and there. And we always do Keith Whitley songs, and people love it. It's not like you get to hear that on the radio anymore, but when they hear their son or daughter, like Georgette, it's like they're actually experiencing it again from that person. I also like to be able to go down and play at these bars, and people will come up and say "Can you please play a Keith Whitley song?" and then I'll pull a real old one out and sing it. And they'll go "OH MY GOD… that's one of my favorites!" That's the greatest, right there!

9

Are there any favorite stories that you have been told about your father you would like to share?

You remember Lefty Frizzell? Well, my dad was a huge Lefty fan… he loved Lefty. He use to do an impersonation of Lefty, and people couldn't tell whether it was my dad or Lefty. He had a message machine on this phone that he recorded that sounded like Lefty: "Keith isn't home right now." And people couldn't tell the difference. I think my uncle was the only one that knew it wasn't Lefty. It was pretty funny. There're a lot of videos out there of Dad impersonating Lefty, and it's quite the comedic thing.

and just walk up and start crying. It's such a cool thing, and I am so thrilled that so many people are still touched by his music.

10

Do you have a website or Facebook page you would like fans to go to?

I do have a Facebook page: Jesse Keith Whitley. And also I am on Instagram… I love Instagram… it's my thing. Both are "Jesse Keith Whitley".

You know, it's cool for me at 28 years old, seeing how much my dad impacts people. People still get emotional. People will come to my mom's show, and they will come up to the merchandise line, and then they'll see me standing there

Kim Brown

1

The new Country Music Entertainers will leave a different kind of *Legacy* than your father had the opportunity to leave. How comfortable do you feel with today's Country Music?

Hmm… that's interesting.

Historically speaking, I think that there have always been people who have been more traditional than contemporary. However, I also feel like there has to be room for both. But that's my opinion. I'm not a person who says "this is Country music, and if you're not creating good sound, then you are not Country". I feel like there has to be room for growth and room for change. I am a person who likes change, and I enjoy how Country Music cycles. You can always find traditional Country and contemporary, and I like it all.

2

As a child of a Country Music legend, what do you feel was the biggest event or experience that impacted *you* the most growing up?

You know, I could answer that in a lot of different ways. But when I really think about having him as my dad, and what that meant to me… he

Jim Ed

always put his family first. He put me first. If we were going to some event that he had to be at, and it was really important and I would say "Dad, I don't know if kids should be here", he would say, "If you're not welcome, I'm not welcome." He always made be feel important, and that had a huge impact on my self-esteem. It helped me to just see myself as being important

to change the oil in my car. I learned how to change tires. Before I was allowed to leave my house after I got my drivers license, I had to learn how to change the tires on every car in the driveway. So he was very present, even though he may not have always been home when I got home from school. I don't look back on my life growing up and not see him being a part of it.

3

Let's talk more about your life behind the curtain. So many of the Country singers were on the road most of the time. Share with me life at home with or without your father. How did that form your life's decisions and path?

Kids always ask me "What was it like to have a dad who was famous?" And I always ask back "What's it like to have a dad who is home every day?" I have nothing to compare it to. When dad was home, he was home, and we had quality time with him. When he was gone, he was gone, and life went on. We just went on with our routine. But I learned so much from my dad. I learned how

4

What single song was your favorite? Why?

Well this will make me cry. I love *"You're The Part Of Me"*. I loved his voice on that song., but I also loved what it meant. I also love *"Scarlet Ribbons"*. And when I was little, before I knew really what it meant, *"Southern Loving"* was my favorite. In the summertime, I would go on the road with him. He would always ask "What do you want me to sing tonight?" And then I would always say *"Southern Loving"*. However, when I got older and listened to the lyrics I was like… Oh, WOW! That's not a good song for a little kid. Haha.

But my favorite song is *"You're The Part Of Me"*.

What other entertainers were you close to growing up? Who hung around your house?

You know, I always went to the Opry with Dad, so nobody ever really hung out. I mean, they would have the Eatin'-Meetin' parties at the house, but I was already older by that time. I loved Roy Acuff, and at the Opry I would sit and talk to him. I loved Jeannie Seely... I loved Johnny Russell... I loved all of them. I don't really remember. I think I took it for granted. I was real busy as a kid; I showed horses and danced. It was a busy house. There could have been people in and out, and I never would have known.

In the story of *your* life, what memories do you have of holidays and special events with your father?

Wow, it's so fresh... does everybody cry when they answer these questions?

Probably too many to list. Christmas was always his very favorite. My birthday is on July 4th, so that was a national holiday. And I was always on the road with him in July. I think I was 7 or 8 before I realized that the fireworks were really NOT for me. We would be at a carnival or something, and they would shoot off fireworks for the 4th of July, and he would say he'd had them do that just for me! But Christmas was his favorite. One Christmas, when I was young, I said that I didn't believe in Santa Claus. He just said "You know... if you don't believe in Santa Claus, he's not going to come and visit you." And I said "Ya ya ya... WHATEVER." I have an older brother who is six years older than me, so I told him, "I know who Santa Claus is," but dad insisted, "If you don't believe, he's not coming." So on Christmas Eve, I went to sleep, woke up early the next morning, and went downstairs. I saw all these presents for my brother, and none for me, and I was just devastated! My brother came downstairs and told me, "You better go back upstairs and tell Santa that you believe. Maybe he hasn't gone that far." So I went upstairs and cried and cried, and I said "I believe... I believe... I believe in Santa Claus," until I'd cried myself to sleep. About an hour later, I woke up and went downstairs, and there were all MY presents, waiting under the tree. And it's funny, 'cause Dad always said that it never happened. He would say, "I don't know what you're talking about." Haha. But he loved Christmas, and it DID happen!

7

I love dogs and had a blonde Cocker Spaniel growing up. Please tell me about *your* pets, if any, or *your* pet as a child.

We had a dog named Gypsy, and many cats and horses. We also had this blue and gold Macaw bird that was a real pain in the rear end. We had to pass him around the family, 'cause he was so annoying. Every couple of years, he would come back to us with new words. One time, Bonnie and Brownie kept him for a couple of years, and he came back with a slightly more colorful vocabulary. When Maxine would go over to their house and walk by the

cage, she would whisper to the bird "You S___ A_ ". So then, when the bird came back home to us and anyone would walk by the cage, the bird would whisper "You S A ." People would do a double-take and ask "Did that bird just say that to me?" Thank you, Maxine!

8

Explain to me how you were able to share *your* musical talents with your father. If not, how have you shared your talents with his fans?

I recorded a little bit, and I used to do a duet when he was really desperate. Let me tell you, it's not any fun to sing *"Lying in Bed With You"* with your dad. So I tried not to do that. I was a professional dancer who could sing a little. I was never really a singer who could dance. I couldn't sing through my nose.

9

What do you miss most about your father?

I don't think that I could say that there is just one thing that

I miss the most, 'cause we were so close. I especially miss the way he was always so excited to see me, and so excited to hear my voice if I called him. If he called me and got my voicemail, he would leave me a message saying "It just makes my day better to get to hear your voice, even if it is voice mail." He was the most loving, sweetest person that anybody could ever know. I miss his happiness. He was always the guy to call if you needed something. He would drop whatever he was doing and be there. It didn't matter what it was; he would be there.

10

Do you have a website or Facebook page you would like to share?

He has a Facebook page but that's all right now.

Steve *Kilgore*

1

The new Country Music Entertainers will leave a different kind of *Legacy* than your father had the opportunity to leave. How comfortable do you feel with today's Country Music?

Well I tell you, I'm not comfortable with today's Country music at all. As a matter of fact, I have started my own record label called Kilgore Country, just for the fact that everybody I meet and talk to go… "That Country ain't Country anymore". On our label, all we do is record real Country music like it used to be.

2

As a child of a Country Music legend, what do you feel was the biggest event or experience that impacted *you* the most growing up?

You're going to be surprised by the answer. I am a magician. I do magic. That's what I do for a living. When I was 6 years old, my dad was doing a show with a professional magician, who was also a promoter and Country music booker. They had a show where it was half Country music, which was my dad, and the other half was magic. Well when I was 6 years old, there were no magicians

Merle

on TV, and I had never heard of or seen a magician. So when I went and saw the show with dad singing, and the guy, Buster Doss, came out and did all that magic, I thought the guy had just walked on water. Everything that I was seeing, I believed was real. Then we were friends with Buster, and he would come over to the house, and he would show me sleight of hand and give me a few magic tricks. I basically got started when I was 6 years old, and have been a magician all my life. That one event, going to that show, would have been the biggest impact.

<h1 style="text-align:center">3</h1>

Let's talk more about your life behind the curtain. So many of the Country singers were on the road most of the time. Share with me life at home with or without your father. How did that form your life's decisions and path?

You are absolutely right. My dad was always on the road, and he was always gone. Dad went on the road with Hank Williams, Jr. when Hank was 8 years old. He was always gone, and then when he came

home he was so exhausted that, for the first day, he was sleeping and trying to catch back up on everything. It was kinda difficult, but nothing as a Country music kid was normal. There was no such thing as going to PTA meetings. We never even had a bedtime. It was just when you passed out, and that was it.

What single song was your favorite? Why?

"Ring of Fire" is definitely our favorite. It's approaching 100 million in sales, and a lot of people don't realize that it was one of the most successful Country music records of all time. Johnny Cash really helped that song as much as anything, and it was a signature song for Johnny... and of course, I love *"Woverton Mountain"* too. I actually knew Clifton Clowers... he was my uncle, so that was always a favorite too.

5

What other entertainers were you close to growing up? Who hung around your house?

Oh… that's an easy answer. Lefty Frizzell. Lefty was our dearest friend, and we loved Lefty and his wife Alice. My sister married Lefty's son, Ricky. And his other son, Marlin, was my best friend. We were always either at their house, or they were at our house. When I was 15, Lefty passed away, but I had known him for a good five years before that happened. What was really cool was that Lefty loved magic tricks, and with me being a magician, I would always show him magic tricks. Lefty liked to fool around, like he could do a little magic; and because I taught him, he never treated me like I was a kid. I was always treated like a friend. That was our special bond. I actually own Lefty Frizzell's guitar, the one he performed with, and it's on loan to the Country Music Hall of Fame. Lefty was the essence of a Country Music Star.

6

In the story of *your* life, what memories do you have of holidays and special events with your father?

Well, when we had Christmas… I don't know if it was because my dad had money or if it was because he felt guilty, but we had *huge* Christmases. I mean embarrassing, *huge* Christmases. In fact, we would have more toys than any other kids on the block.

Dad had a little dog that he loved to death. You know how when folks ask at Christmas "what do you give a man that has everything in the world?" It's difficult, and there was a little pressure as to what to get dad. Well, this one year I found a water fountain for dogs at a pet center. It sort of recirculated the water. I gave that to dad, and he said it was the best Christmas present he'd gotten.

7

I love dogs and had a blonde Cocker Spaniel growing up. Please tell me about *your* pets, if any, or *your* pet as a child.

We love animals and we always had dogs. Being a magician, I had a bird, "Howard the Wonder Dove", that worked with me in my magic act. And he lived to be 23 years old. The vet who gave it to me chronicled his life, and he would write stories. The average life in the wild is about two years, so this one living for twenty-three years was something. I retired him after ten years, and then he was just a family pet. He never saw another bird. It was really weird.

8

Explain to me how you were able to share *your* musical talents with your father. If not, how have you shared your talents with his fans?

I share some of my stories about going up Kilgore. I write for magazine called *The Nashville Music Guy,* and always write stories about my dad on Facebook. People are always encouraging me to write a book, but I am a magician, and I go out and mention my father during my magic shows. We also have a publishing company called *More and*

More Music. My dad's first hit was *More and More.* It was recorded by Web Pierce and sold a million copies. Mickey Gilley cut it; Elvis Costello cut it and sold 2 ½ million.

9

What do you miss most about your father?

Everything.

10

Do you have a website or Facebook page you would like to share?

Kilgorecompany.com

Jett Williams

1

The new Country Music Entertainers will leave a different kind of *Legacy* than your father had the opportunity to leave. How comfortable do you feel with today's Country Music?

Today's Country music is a different kind of Country music than the traditional Country music. I don't consider it real Country; I think that it's taken a turn more toward the Pop side of music.

2

You did not know you were the daughter of Hank Williams until you were an adult. What was the biggest event or story about your father that impacted you the most?

The most important thing that impacted me *personally* was that my father went to the attorneys, trying to get a pre-birth custody contract. He not only said that he was my father, but that he wanted me. That's what convinced me that he was my father.

Hank

3

Both of my children are adopted. How has the journey to obtain your birthright impacted your views on adoption?

Adoption is two sides of the same coin. You know, 'cause the mother has the right to privacy, but the children also have the right to know. So it's one of those old-age questions that will never be answered, and it's really hard to have to put a universal answer on it. Each and every circumstance is different, along with the personalities of the folks involved.

4

Let's talk more about your life behind the curtain. So many of the Country singers were on the road most of the time and were not home for their kids birthdays and special occasions. How was your life growing up? What were your birthdays and holidays like?

I didn't grow up in entertainment, or with a parent in Country music, so my situation was completely different. I didn't grow up the same way that they did, but I know a lot of the "kids", and they grew up knowing that they were the children of Country music stars, and that their mom or dad weren't going to be home, and they knew that they would miss holidays. You know, it's like if you have a job and happen to be overseas as a soldier; you may not be home for holidays. There are other professions, including the military, where children's parents may not be home for their birthdays, anniversaries and Christmas. Also, how successful you are depends on how much you are on the road.

5

What single song of your father's is your favorite? Why?

My personal favorite song is "I'm So Lonesome I Could Cry". I just believe that it is the most perfect lyrical song.

6

What other entertainers have reached out to you? Do you hang with any of them?

I have been fortunate enough to be friends with a lot of them, like Loretta Lynn and Billy Walker. When I entered the Country music scene, George Jones reached out and had me on his shows. Chet Atkins was very good to me as well. I was very fortunate to have good friendships.

7

In the story of *your* life, if your father had not died, how do you believe he would have written your story?

I don't ever address that, because whatever is… is, and there's no reason to speculate on what would have been.

8

I love dogs and had a blonde Cocker Spaniel growing up. Please tell me about *your* pets, if any, or *your* pet as a child.

Growing up, I always had a dog. Now I have a dog, a cat, mules and horses.

9

Explain to me how sharing your talents with your father's fans have impacted you?

Sharing my father's music and legacy with his fans has allowed me to bond with them and to make good friendships. I honor them for loving my dad and by getting to meet their child and grandchildren. Fans were very warm and receptive after learning about my existence. The other thing about me being able to tour is that I think, for the fans, it was like "Oh my gosh, there's a little bit more of the pie." The fact that I looked just like him was pretty much a giveaway.

10

What would you say to your father today if you had the opportunity?

I love you.

11

Have you seen your father's new movie, "I Saw the Light"? What are your thoughts?

I think that Tom Hiddleston did a great job. I also think the other actors and actresses did a great job. It's pretty hard to write conversations about something that you weren't privy to. And that's not just this movie, but movies about people's lives. If you weren't in the room, then you wouldn't know exactly what was said. I did spend one day on the set during the filming in Shreveport.

12

Do you have a website or Facebook page you would like to share?

Jettwilliams.com

Facebook fanpage is updated daily/weekly.

Photos courtesy of Jett Williams Productions.

Julie *Husky*

1

The new Country Music Entertainers will leave a different kind of *Legacy* than your father had the opportunity to leave. How comfortable do you feel with today's Country Music?

Today's Country music has much to offer in a category all of its own, not to be confused with the Classic Country of yesteryear. I hold a great deal of respect for the past and present trailblazers, as long as honor and decency are upheld.

2

As a child of a Country Music legend, what do you feel was the biggest event or experience that impacted *you* the most growing up?

We Husky kids inherited my dad's sense of humor and quick wit. Our dad gave us the gift of laughter. For example, Dad's philosophy on furniture dusting was "You have to wipe the dust off *before* you spray the polish… otherwise, it just makes mud!"

Ferlin

3

Let's talk more about your life behind the curtain. So many of the Country singers were on the road most of the time. Share with me life at home with or without your father. How did that form your life's decisions and path?

Dad had congestive heart failure and chronic heart issues throughout his life, which prevented him from many career opportunities. He traveled frequently, and our biggest fear was to hear on the news that he had died from a heart attack during a show or appearance away from home. Dad never lost faith in God, and we treasured his Christian influence on us. The good Lord was kind enough to allow us all to be at his bedside when he passed from this world into the next.

4

What single song was your favorite? Why?

"Wings of a Dove" is the iconic favorite, the most recognizable, and also featured

in the Oscar-winning Robert Duvall movie *"Tender Mercies"*. I'd have to go with that one.

5

What other entertainers were you close to growing up? Who hung around your house?

My dad took in Dallas Frazier at the tender age of 12 and helped raise him. Tommy Collins (Merle Haggard's "Leonard") hung out with us a lot, along with Johnny Russell, George Jones, Waylon Jennings, Jean Shepard and Sheb Wooley. When my brother Danny was killed in a car accident in 1970, Johnny Cash was the first person at our door to comfort and console our family.

6

In the story of *your* life, what memories do you have of holidays and special events with your father?

Dad LOVED Christmas. He always made the holidays memorable with a warm fire in the fireplace, a big pot of chili cooking on the stove, and lots of family time together. Christmas Eve at our house was always filled with laughter, music, fellowship and Ferlin's chili… a tradition that we carry on and preserve to this day.

7

I love dogs and had a blonde Cocker Spaniel growing up. Please tell me about *your* pets, if any, or *your* pet as a child.

We had a red Dachshund named "Winnie the Pooch", affectionately addressed as "Pooh Dog", and a beautiful Siberian Husky that Dad had cleverly named "Yksuh" ("Husky" spelled backwards).

8

Explain to me how you were able to share *your* musical talents with your father. If not, how have you shared your talents with his fans?

I love music, and I loved to sing with Dad on many occasions. As for sharing my talents with his fans, I can't

take credit for anything other than just being born, and I can only be proud of who my Dad was, and of the legacy he left behind on this world. I also work at Husky Music, Inc., my Dad's music publishing company, in the hopes of continuing to share his music and songwriting compositions with the world.

9

What do you miss most about your father?

Like clockwork, my dad would always call us on our birthdays and sing Happy Birthday (deliberately off-key) in his voice of Simon Crum. As corny and ridiculous as it was to me then, I would give anything to wake up on any given birthday today and hear his lovable, silly voice again.

10

Do you have a website or Facebook page you would like to share?

Yes, ferlinhusky.com and Ferlin Husky & Simon Crum on Facebook.

Melissa *Luman*

1

The new Country Music Entertainers will leave a different kind of *Legacy* than your father had the opportunity to leave. How comfortable do you feel with today's Country Music?

Not comfortable at all... I think that today's Country music has lost the feel, the emotion... the reason behind the song.

2

As a child of a Country Music legend, what do you feel was the biggest event or experience that impacted *you* the most growing up?

My dad passed away when I was 12 years old; so, growing up, I was so young that I really didn't quite understand the exalted company that I was in when my dad would say, "Come on, Melissa, we gotta go to the Opry." I'd be running around backstage and getting in all kinds of trouble... but I guess, looking back now, that going to the Opry was the greatest thing, growing up in that kind of household.

3

Let's talk more about your life behind the curtain. So many of the Country singers

Bob

were on the road most of the time. Share with me life at home with or without your father. How did that form your life's decisions and path?

Well, I'm an only child, and my dad was on the road all the time. And when he wasn't on the road, he was at the Opry on Friday and Saturday night. Of course, back then, they had to fulfill their number of weekends that they performed. So when he wasn't on the road, he was on the Opry, and when he wasn't on the road or the Opry, he was at the country club playing golf, or in his garden. So of course my mother and I were very close, with me being the only child. But whenever my dad was home, he and I did things together that stick out in my mind. Being in my 50s now, I am rather independent.

4

What single song was your favorite? Why?

He had a bunch that I really, really love, but what I guess I have to say is probably *"Lonely Women Make Good Lovers"*, 'cause that put a lot of clothes on our back.

5

What other entertainers were you close to growing up? Who hung around your house?

Well, I grew up on Caudill Drive, so our next-door neighbors were Roy Orbison, Johnny Cash, and Helen Carter (I called them Mama and Papa Cash). So I grew up in a subdivision where I was surrounded by that kind of entertainment, and they were always in and out of the house. Of course, Roy Orbison took me home from the bus stop. I went to a private school, and at the private school there were lots of us "Nashville Brats", as I like to call them. There was me and Bobby Jr., John Carter Cash, some of the Orbison kids, Matt Dodney (Barbara Mandrell's son); and Dr Hook, his daughter went to school with us. So we were around them growing up... one big family.

6

In the story of *your* life, what memories do you have of holidays and special events with your father?

My mother was a wonderful, wonderful picture-taker, and she had photo albums done by the dates and by the holidays. So I have pictures with my dad, pictures of my stockings, my presents, and my Christmas trees. So those memories stand out in my mind wonderfully.

7

I love dogs and had a blonde Cocker Spaniel growing up. Please tell me about *your* pets, if any, or *your* pet as a child.

I had tons of pets of growing up. I had two horses, and I had dogs: Tippy, Suzie, Archie and Petunia. Petunia was actually brought home by my dad in his pocket. He brought her home and surprised my mom with her. He had always talked about wanting a monkey, and my mom was always scared that he would come home one day with a monkey. So he did come home one day and say "... Well, I got that monkey that I always wanted." Then he pulled out of his pocket a 2 lb. Teacup Peke-a-poo, Petunia.

I do have a dog now, a Boston Terrier, and she is my child.

8

Explain to me how you were able to share *your* musical talents with your father. If not, how have you shared your talents with his fans?

Well, the way that I share it now, I owe it all to Robyn Young. I had always sung when I was younger, but that was when I was in college and I really wasn't 110% ready to put it out there. So I kinda let it go by the wayside. Robyn called me and said, *"Hey, we're filming this show. You want to do it?"* And of course I said yes before he'd even finished his sentence. Thank goodness for Larry Black and his wonderful show.

We now get together and call ourselves the *Nashville Brat Pack*. We all get together and do shows around town. Some of us have gone out of town and done shows. We just sing the songs that made our parents famous, and fans love it.

9

What do you miss most about your father?

I just miss my father... I don't know what I miss most. I just miss him.

10

Do you have a website or Facebook page you would like to share?

Next Generation: Sons & Daughters of Country Legends.

Sharon
ilburn

1

The new Country Music Entertainers will leave a different kind of *Legacy* than your father had the opportunity to leave. How comfortable do you feel with today's Country Music?

Not good. I don't think Country Music is Country Music any more. It may even be a dying art, unless we get some real gems back into the program. In the older generation of Country, we felt like we were all family. There wasn't a time when people didn't respond, to... "I'm in town, I'm ready to do the Opry." Now, people don't do that. People don't show up... they don't call like they should. They figure that they are off the road and they don't have an endeavor to undertake. And if we are going to keep Country going the way that it's always been, then we need people to step up to the plate and make that happen.

2

As a child of a Country Music legend, what do you feel was the biggest event or experience that impacted *you* the most growing up?

Going to sleep under the recording booth at the "Quonset Hut" recording studio started by Owen

Doyle

Bradley. My dad or my mom would be recording late, and I remember going to sleep on the sofa, or even in the floor while they were recording. I remember it as if it was yesterday. I got to hear so many different entertainers record… you know, my dad was in on Loretta's start and her first record deal. So my childhood was spent being around all the people that I really took for granted.

me. That's not to say I didn't learn anything from my mom, 'cause I did… but I spent so much time with my grandmother, and she and I were so close that she had the biggest influence on my life. That was a peak time for my dad, so he was gone a lot. But when he was home, entertainers would show up at any given time. They might write, or sit and talk about music, and my mother would cook these big breakfasts in the wee hours of the morning. It was an amazing life.

3

Let's talk more about your life behind the curtain. So many of the Country singers were on the road most of the time. Share with me life at home with or without your father. How did that form your life's decisions and path?

Oh my gosh… my grandmother, my dad's mother, they always referred to her as "Mom Wilburn" and dedicated something to her at every performance. She was a profound influence on my life. I learned a lot of my cooking techniques, a lot of my cleaning, my ironing, my washing… you name it, I learned it from her. She had the most influence on

4

What single song was your favorite? Why?

There are two that really stick out in my mind. One is *"Medals for Mothers"*… and I guess that had the most visual effect on my life, because I could almost see my grandmother receiving medals in heaven when she got there.

And the other one was "The Old Folks Home". My dad was fantastic at recitation. That one showed me that you don't ever just put your family into an old folks' home and discard them. It's your responsibility to take care of them, because they took care of you.

5

What other entertainers were you close to growing up? Who hung around your house?

Roger Miller, Willie Nelson… gosh, I can't even name them all. We were with Roy Acuff a lot, and with Bill Anderson. He lived just around the corner from where we lived. There were so many people, and if they weren't at my house, they were over at my Granny's house. And my Granny would be cooking all these meals. I think that just about everyone from that generation, at one time or another, has sat at one table or the other.

Did Doyle and Teddy hang out together when they weren't on the road?

They didn't really hang out that much, because they were together all the time on the road. They would call each other, and of course dad was the one who always chose what was going to be sung on what show and helped with the booking. And Teddy always chose what outfits to wear. So it just kinda worked like a clock. Everything that they did, from the way they started playing to start a show to the bow to the audience, was done with such precision that it was as if they were one. So except for the holidays, I can't ever remember them just hanging out.

6

In the story of *your* life, what memories do you have of holidays and special events with your father?

Well, we would ALL (the whole family) always go to Granny's and have a big meal, no matter what the holiday was. Dad was generally in charge of watermelon-cutting. He would cut 'em up, and then us kids would eat watermelon and have seed-spitting contests. And then all the cousins would play hide and seek until we were played out. The adults would do the cooking and cleaning. It was all fond, fond memories, and I can't think of a time that any of us didn't meet there for a holiday and enjoy it. When Granny died, the family kinda split apart and started doing their own things.

7

I love dogs and had a blonde Cocker Spaniel growing up. Please tell me about *your* pets, if any, or *your* pet as a child.

Oh yes… I had two that really stand out. My first when I was little was a German Shepherd that I named Whoa Whoa… because I thought that in the song that went "Put it off until tomorrow, whoa… whoa…", I thought they were talking about a dog. So that's what I named my dog. Then my dad got me a housedog that was a little black Poodle, and I named him Teddy, after Uncle Ted. I had Teddy for a long time, and he was in fact on the TV show some with Teddy's Collie named Silver. And I loved that dog like my own, because I spent so much time with my grandmother.

When I was growing up, at age 13 I decided that I wanted to be a singer, but they wouldn't let me. They were determined that I would finish school, which I did. I was always in the talent shows, school productions and musicals, and I remember my dad and Teddy being at the high school talent show that I actually ended up winning. I did a medley of Crystal Gayle songs, and I think my dad was most impressed by that performance on the talent show my junior year than he was at any other time. I sang on their TV show, and I danced some… and I was on the swing set during one of the segments. I sang on the Opry with them sometimes. We decided to do a generation show at Fan Fair one year, with me and my parents, but Teddy was in the audience and couldn't stand it… so he had to come up on stage and sing with us too.

8

Explain to me how you were able to share *your* musical talents with your father. If not, how have you shared your talents with his fans?

9

What do you miss most about your father?

Everything. There are so many times since he's been gone that I wish that I could just have a moment. "Daddy, I need to talk to you"… "This is going on"… *You are going to make me cry…* "I don't know how to handle this situation"… "I really could use your input". And my dad was so intelligent when it came to business decisions, so I really miss those times to talk with him.

10

Do you have a website or Facebook page you would like to share?

No… I don't have a fan page… just family.

We do have a Wilburn Brothers Facebook Page that fans can go to.

My dad was a great man, and he died way too soon. Teddy was lost when he died, even though he continued to perform. Every time he would perform, I could hear my dad with him. I really miss him.

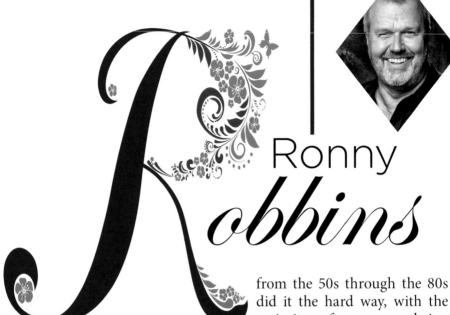

Ronny Robbins

1

The new Country Music Entertainers will leave a different kind of *Legacy* than your father had the opportunity to leave. How comfortable do you feel with today's Country Music?

I think Tracy Lawrence sang it best when he recorded "Time Marches On", and I don't think that today's crop of artists will be that memorable five years from now, just as there are a lot of artists from ten years ago whom you seldom hear from today. Every generation has its own brand of music, and the artists that have left a legacy from the 50s through the 80s did it the hard way, with the majority of exposure being 100,000 miles a year playing those night clubs and concert venues. It would take years to build a following that way, but the end product came in the form of fans that would give a lifetime of loyalty to an artist. With the advent of electronic media, an artist can reach more people in a 24-hour period than in six months on the road, but the downside to me is that you are not going be able to establish an artist/fan relationship before the next big thing comes down the road. Of course there are always exceptions, but in general, today's buying public has so many choices that it all comes down to who has the best marketability, as it is as much about image as it is about the music.

Marty

2

As a child of a Country Music legend, what do you feel was the biggest event or experience that impacted *you* the most growing up?

First off, I don't think I ever thought of him as a legend growing up. Even though he was probably in his best years in the 60s, those were pretty turbulent times growing up as a teenager. The early R&B influence, the Beatles, Stones and all of the protest movements of the late 60s didn't leave a lot of room in a teenager's addled brain, and Dad was gone so much in those years that I was much more influenced by local Rock & Roll radio and participation in a series of garage bands (we called them combos back then… not sure why…I think maybe it was because so many of the guys would be playing in two or three different bands, which would make for an interesting combination of players, depending on who would actually have a paying gig on any given weekend).

3

Let's talk more about your life behind the curtain. So many of the Country singers were on the road most of the time. Share with me life at home with or without your father. How did that form your life's decisions and path?

I can't say I gave it much thought at the time. It was just a fact of life that Dad was going to be gone a lot of time throughout the year, and especially during the summer months. That changed a little when Dad started racing, as he was then able to adjust his schedule so that he could race at the Fairgrounds Speedway on Saturday night. That really worked out well, since the Opry had an extra half-hour segment on the second show at 11:30, and he could race earlier in the evening. Those were some of my best memories growing up, because we always saw eye-to-eye when it came to racing. We seldom, if ever, agreed on music, as the lines between Country and Rock in the 60s were as distinct as mustard and mayonnaise - although, unbeknownst to him, I probably knew over a hundred Country songs at the time, and just never had the opportunity to sing them. I was playing electric keyboard in the last band I was in, we were doing good dance music, Sam & Dave, James Brown, Wilson Pickett stuff, but we were losing gigs because everything was going psychedelic, strobe light druggy music. I was just knocking around on the keyboard one night and Dad came in, and he was really complimenting my playing, it took me totally off-guard. I told him how tired I was getting of the changes in our audience. He told me that if I would learn three Country songs, he would put me on his road show. I just kind of chuckled to myself and whipped out "You Win Again", "No One Will Ever Know", and "I Couldn't Keep From Crying" for him. He had no way of backing out then... he had to hire me. Haha.

4

What single song was your favorite? Why?

I don't have any one favorite. It kind of depends on the mood I'm in, but he did a couple of songs, *"Man Walks Among Us"* and *"My Love"*, that are both talking about the wide open spaces and man's encroachment

building bigger cities, roads, etc. Just simple songs that I know meant something to him when he wrote them. Neither was a big hit, they were just nice, beautiful songs. I think Dad wrote "Man Walks Among Us" specifically with Phoenix in mind, places where I learned to drive while Dad was in the back seat with a .22, shooting rabbits for his Mom.

5

What other entertainers were you close to growing up? Who hung around your house?

There really weren't that many, although Eddy and Sally Arnold would come over for Mexican food on occasion. Dad would always bring Mexican food supplies home whenever he toured out west; there wasn't much available in the grocery stores back in the 50s. Little Roy Wiggins and family used to come over quite a bit, as well as Brenda Lee on occasion. She brought Ronnie over one time and introduced him as her fiancé. I went to my room and cried my eyes out. I'd assumed that since she and I were the same height we must be about the same age, and I knew that she must love me because I could tell by the way she ignored me… haha. I'm not even exactly sure how old I was.

6

In the story of *your* life, what memories do you have of holidays and special events with your father?

My biggest memory, I suppose, is that Dad was always careful to never get booked on or around Christmas, and on most Thanksgivings. Many years, we would go back to Phoenix, as Mom and Dad's siblings were - for the most part - still in the Phoenix area, so there were cousins galore, and just some great family times. The years that we stayed in Nashville were a lot quieter, but still fun, because it was great to have Dad home and relaxed. Sometimes it would take him 3-4 days to unwind from a trip, but at least during the Christmas season he would carve out 6-7 days on either side.

7

I love dogs and had a blonde Cocker Spaniel growing up. Please tell me about *your* pets, if any, or *your* pet as a child.

My first pet was a Collie named Mickey. We got him shortly after we moved to Nashville in January of '53. At least, we always referred to him as a Collie, even though he really didn't look that much like Lassie. He was a great dog though, and lived to be almost 14 years old.

8

Explain to me how you were able to share *your* musical talents with your father. If not, how have you shared your talents with his fans?

I was fortunate enough to tour some with my dad. And since his passing, I manage "Marty Robbins Enterprises". I have also been on some of the Country Family Reunion and Larry's Country Diner shows, plus the Cruises. Those shows give me another platform to share his memory and music with his fans.

9

What do you miss most about your father?

Everything, but probably the biggest thing was growing older with him. He was only 57 when he died; I was 33. I'm 66 as of this writing, and Dad would have turned 90 on 9-26-2015. I hate that he never saw his grandchildren, or his great granddaughter, although he was so sensitive about his age. He never would have admitted at the time that he was a grand-dad.

10

Do you have a website or Facebook page you would like to share?

We just recently started a page on Facebook, "Marty Robbins Enterprises".

About the Author

enae Johnson lives in Nashville, Tennessee and although she does not claim the title "author," she has written three books. And although she does not claim the title "waitress", she plays one on the hit TV show, *Larry's Country Diner*. And although she does not claim to be related or married to Larry Black, creator of *Country's Family Reunion* and *Larry's Country Diner* TV shows, she has worked with him for over 18 years. Thus being nicknamed "his office wife" by his real wife, Luann.

Renae gives Larry credit for seeing her creative talents and the opportunity to accomplish what ever she sets her mind to. Her energy mixed with hard work and her expertise in customer service and marketing has been a real asset to further her career.

One of the special talents Renae has is to embrace people. Whether it is at the offices of Gabriel Communications, Larry's Country Diner, Starlite Theater, Larry's Country Diner and Country's Family Reunion Cruise or just a visit to Wal-Mart she greets folks with a smile and a hug.

Diary of a TV Waitress was written specially for the fans of the hit TV show *Larry's Country Diner*. It answers many of the questions fans have asked about the cast and show over the years. *Precious Memories Memorial* was written especially for the fans of the TV series *Country's Family Reunion* and real traditional country music fans. It answers many of the questions fans have ask about the Country Music Legends careers, deaths, celebration of life and final resting places. It covers over 80 legends from Roy Acuff to Jim Ed Brown. *Precious Memories Legacy* was written out of love for these beautiful kids of the Country Music Legends who scarified so much for us. So she embraced them with this book to honor them.

On a personal note:

Renae is married to Dove Award and Grammy Nominated Christian record producer and writer, Phil Johnson. They have one daughter, Chi who is a professional dancer with an impressive resume that includes touring with Paul McCartney. Her husband, Elliott also works for Gabriel Communications as Social Media consultant. Renae is a proud grandma of two beautiful granddaughters, Rio and Sedona, who show up at the Diner occasionally. Justin, Renae's son was killed in an automobile accident on Cool Springs Blvd on New Years morning 2008 on his way to work. He was 28.